27
12/04

P9-AQU-459

THE CELTIC COLLECTION

2100357

THE CELTIC COLLECTION

TWENTY-FIVE
★ KNITWEAR ★
DESIGNS FOR
MEN AND WOMEN

★ ALICE ★
STARMORE

Butler Area Public Library
218 North McKean Street
Butler, PA 16001

Trafalgar Square Publishing

746.43
STA

First published in the United States of America
in 1993 by Trafalgar Square Publishing,
North Pomfret, Vermont 05053
First paperback edition 1994
Reprinted 1996, 1997, 1998, 2000

Printed in Singapore by Imago

Originally published by Anaya Publishers Ltd, London

Text copyright © Alice Starmore 1992
Photography copyright © Anaya Publishers Ltd 1992
except for picture credited on page 144
The designs in this publication may not be knitted for resale.

Editor Margaret Maino
Designer David Fordham
Photographer Mike Bunn
Stylist Karen Harrison
Pattern Checker Marilyn Wilson
Chartist Tessa Dennison
Knitting Techniques Illustrator Conny Jude

All rights reserved.
No part of this publication may be reproduced, stored in a retrieval system, or
transmitted, in any form or by any means, electronic, mechanical,
photocopying, recording or otherwise, without the prior permission of the
copyright holder.

Library of Congress Catalog Card Number: 94-60160

ISBN 1-57076-005-5
Typeset in Great Britain by Bookworm Typesetting, Manchester
Colour reproduction by J. Film Process, Singapore

CONTENTS

INTRODUCTION

THE CELTIC PEOPLE

'THEY WEAR ORNAMENTS of gold, torques on their necks, and bracelets on their arms and wrists, while people of high rank wear dyed garments besprinkled with gold.' A quotation by Strabo, the Greek geographer and historian writing in Rome between 60BC and AD23, aptly describes the Celtic people.

There is a group of Britons, just a few thousand in number, with British names and British ancestry stretching back across centuries, who nonetheless did not learn English as their first language. I am one of them, and in common with many others of my generation from the Isle of Lewis, one of the group of Western Islands off the north-west coast of Scotland, spoke only Gaelic until I went to school. It was several years before I realized that we were in a tiny minority within the UK. There were others, I learned, who spoke languages related to my own, and occupied similar peripheral positions on the Atlantic seaboard: in Ireland, in Wales and even in Brittany. Together, we make up the distant descendants of the Celts, who could once claim much of Europe as their own.

The term 'Celtic' is inextricably associated with 'twilight', meaning here a race in decline with dying traditions and arts, and a Celtic streak in character often refers to extreme melancholy, or wild self-destructive tendencies. Yet this must be balanced against an undeniable magnificence in the Celtic image. It is perhaps best personified in Boadicea – or more correctly, Boudicca – the warrior Queen of the Iceni, who rebelled against her Roman oppressors in AD60 during the reign of Nero.

She had spirit, the verve, the army, excellent weapons, and right upon her side. Yet she failed, defeated by the smaller army and superior generalship of Suetonius Paulinus. Boudicca took poison rather than accept defeat and humiliation, and now serves as a glorious symbol of Celtic decline, and the paradox of a powerful warrior people, destined to lose. It is not the last paradox that students of the Celtic peoples will encounter.

THE HISTORY OF THE CELTS

Those who seek information on these people will find that almost every book on the subject begins with a statement rather like a disclaimer, outlining the difficulties of defining exactly what 'Celtic' means. The Celts never achieved nationhood, but remained a collection of tribes who warred between themselves. Their rise and fall spans over one thousand years with their peak years between 700BC and AD450, and they covered vast tracts of territory. They were illiterate until their twilight years, and therefore had no written records.

It is accepted that the Celts have their background in Eastern Europe, and achieved the status of an iron-using, farming society by about 700BC. Various tribes spread westwards through Austria, France and the Low Countries before reaching Britain and Ireland by about 250BC. Because they were a non-literary society, our knowledge of them is based on Greek, Roman and Etruscan accounts, and on artefacts from burial chambers and other archaeological sites. This last strand of information is naturally haphazard but has the advantage of providing us with information gained from the Celts themselves, rather than from possibly biased Roman commentators. The buried objects are largely weapons, personal ornaments and drinking vessels, showing them to be a warrior-based society with a fine aesthetic sense. Their metallurgy was state-of-the-art for its day and their artistry and craftsmanship has provided us with some of the finest treasures of the ancient world.

Strabo describes the Celts as physically attractive people – tall, white skinned and fair-haired. Yet, he goes on, they are boasters and threateners fond of bombastic arguments after their communal feasts which often lead to violent single combats. But he also writes of lyric poets called bards, of musicians playing lyre-type instruments, and of honoured philosophers and theologians called Druids. There is undoubtedly the patronizing tone of the conqueror about such descriptions – the problem of history being written by the winners. The Celts did love ornament and display, and their ornaments and workmanship rank among the very best the world has ever seen. They were illiterate but were quick of mind and had a lyric, oral tradition that passed from one generation to the next. Their extravagant personalities probably were childlike to a formal, Roman point of view, but it was balanced by a straightforward way in dealings with other peoples, and therein lay their downfall.

The Celtic culture as based upon the warrior and the display of gorgeous ceremonial weapons was vital to a chieftain. Strabo describes the Celts as, 'madly fond of war, high-spirited and quick to battle, but otherwise straightforward and not of evil character. And so when they are stirred up they assemble in their bands for battle, quite openly and without forethought, so they are easily handled by those who wish to outwit them'. Add their appalling tactical sense to the disparate nature of the Celtic tribes, and we see why they fell easily before the expansionary aims of a disciplined, cohesive Roman Empire. Many Celtic warriors scorned armour and made it a point of honour to fight naked wearing nothing but a metal torque, their hair limed and whitened into peaks. Their tribal leaders were individualists to a degree that precluded any form of nationhood. Boudicca was typical in having the strength and the spirit but no organization.

The British Celts were eclipsed later than their European relatives, but eclipsed they most certainly were. The Romans invaded in AD43 and stayed for 400 years. Even after their withdrawal, a wave of Anglo-Saxon immigrants to Britain continued to subsume what remained of the Celtic population, apart from in the extreme western fringes. Ireland was untouched by the Roman legions and remained a Celtic bastion but from AD432 onwards, Christianity and the Church of Rome managed to succeed where military had failed. Today, just the Celtic Fringe remains although scattered throughout the major museums of Western Europe is a body of work that forms the inspiration for this book.

THE CELTIC LANDSCAPE

The development of Celtic art spans from 500BC to about AD800, including the pagan and Christian eras. Yet throughout these disparate centuries, the broad sweep of Celtic art exudes a magic and mysticism where nothing is fixed, nothing is definite and nothing is exactly as it seems.

The Celts had no written language but their visual images were powerful, evocative and sophisticated – first in metalwork – on weapons, drinking vessels and personal ornaments, usually for the glorification of some local chieftain. The last flowering of Celtic art used illuminated manuscript as its medium, and had quite a different purpose. The gospel of Colmcille – more commonly known as the Book of Kells – was created by monks in the late 8th or early 9th century to celebrate and glorify Christ but the images it uses are as resolutely pagan as any on the shield of a pre-Christian warrior. In the Book of Kells, every Celtic metaphor is employed and given a final polish. Rather than going out with a dying whimper, Celtic art exits with a glorious flourish.

A single page from the Book of Kells (left) illustrates craftsmanship and artistry of the highest order. The execution of detail is so precise, that no one is sure how it was achieved. The monks, in common with the earlier Celtic metalworkers, were masters of their art. The next feature is fluidity of form. A rectilinear border containing precisely executed key patterns and interlacing knotwork, suddenly transmutes into the body of a ferocious dragon-like beast, which closes the border by breathing fire at its own tail. Beside its head, another beast manages – by fantastic contortion – to become the letter T. This balance between nature's chaos and ordered abstraction is absolutely central. Triskel spirals are a similar constant feature throughout centuries of Celtic art, and could symbolize life, death and rebirth.

These glorious images perfectly suit the techniques and practicalities of knitting, and in this book I have used them, taking care to be true to their antecedents. Knotwork patterns are always unbroken, and in two designs – Tara (page 73) and Iona (page 81)– I have focused on the knotwork to produce powerful emblematic symbols. Spirals are used in a formal manner in Armagh (page 111) and Roscrea (page 115), while in Turoe (page 99) and Roineval (page 103) they are deliberately more abstract and enigmatic. The key patterns, with their strong diagonals, are perfect for the Fair Isle technique, and there are several included in this collection. Beasts are allowed to erupt only three times – somewhat playfully on Tipperary (page 127); in a slightly more ferocious manner on Shannon (page 131), and interlaced stealthily in the borders of Erin (page 122).

Working with these symbols has been a personal voyage of discovery. While doing the calculations necessary to turn metalwork, stonework and manuscript into knitting, I developed an admiration for, and empathy with, the elements in the Celtic visual language. I found that they flowed perfectly, I could manipulate them with ease and they made complete visual sense. Whether or not this is due to my Celtic background, I simply do not know. However, through the sweaters in this book, I hope I have made the Celtic landscape come alive and that I have provided a means for its artistic metaphors to leave the museums and be admired and enjoyed in everyday life.

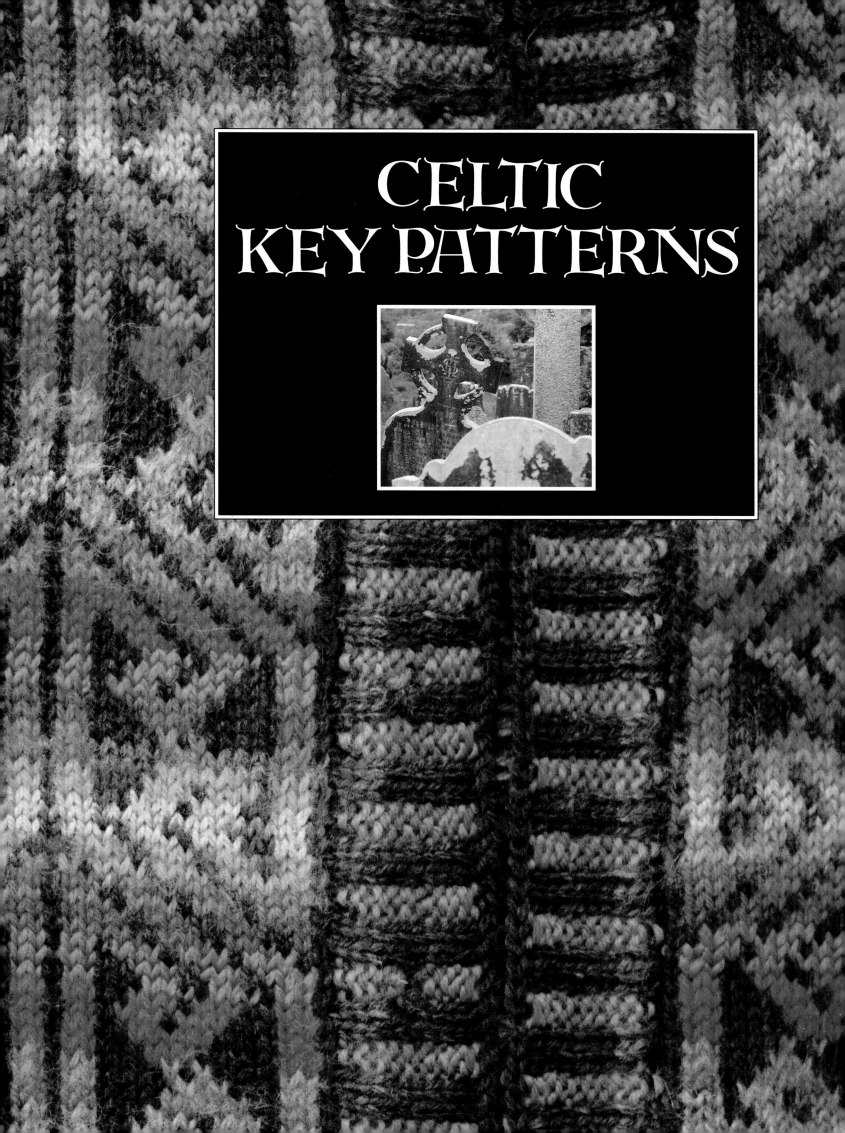

CELTIC
KEY PATTERNS

ALBA
CELTIC KEY SWEATER

RATING

★ ★

SIZES
To fit bust 86-92[94-102]cm 34-36[37-40]in.
Directions for larger size are given in parenthesis. Where there is only one set of figures, it applies to both sizes.

KNITTED MEASUREMENTS
Width underarm 108[119.5]cm 42½[47]in.
Length from top of shoulder 55.5[58.5]cm 21¾[23]in.
Sleeve length 42.5[45]cm 16¾[17¾]in.

MATERIALS
Yarn: Rowan LDK; Rowan Silkstones; Rowan Donegal Tweed; Rowan Wool/Cotton.

A. Dragonfly Silkstones (823) 100g;
B. Mushroom LDK (59) 50g; **C.** Dove Wool/Cotton (911) 40[80]g; **D.** Teal Silkstones (828) 50[100]g; **E.** Kashmir Wool/Cotton (910) 40[80]g; **F.** Dried Rose Silkstones (825) 50g; **G.** Woad Silkstones (829) 50g; **H.** Dusk LDK (423) 25g; **I.** Pale Silver LDK (58) 25[50]g; **J.** Peppermint LDK (416) 50g; **K.** Dolphin Donegal Tweed (478) 50[75]g; **L.** Sea Green LDK (665) 50[75]g; **M.** Aqua LDK (123) 50g; **N.** Beetle Silkstones (834) 50[100]g; **O.** Ice Blue LDK (48) 50g; **P.** Blue Mist Silkstones (832) 50g; **Q.** Mulled Wine Silkstones (830) 50g; **R.** Pale Blue LDK (122) 25g.

1 Set of double-pointed or circular 3¼mm (US3) needles. 2 Stitch holders. 2 Safety pins.

TENSION (GAUGE)
15 sts and 15 rows to 5cm (2in), measured over chart patt, using 3¼mm (US3) needles and working the patt on right side only, breaking off yarns at the end of every row. See page 137 for making a Fair Isle swatch.

The haphazard stacking of logs of peat provides a graphic background for this stunning sweater in many different shades of blue and indigo. A clever two-tone ribbed pattern makes a braided effect for the neck, cuff and lower edgings.

The arrowhead key pattern that I have chosen for this sweater is an example of Pictish Celtic art from the Nigg stone, an ancient stone cross standing in North Eastern Scotland. It is worked here in a blend of eighteen misty shades that are reminiscent of the early morning colours of lakes and distant hills, and complemented by check patterned borders.

STITCHES
Chart patt: K every round, and on two-colour rounds, strand the yarn not in immediate use evenly across wrong side. On stretches of more than 7 sts in one colour, weave in yarn not in use at centre of stretch. **Steeks:** Worked at armholes and neck, and later cut up centre to form openings. The steek is worked over 10 sts. K these sts on every round, and on two-colour rounds, K each st and round in alt colours. Do not weave in newly joined in or broken off yarns at centre of first steek. Instead leave approx. 5cm (2in) tail when joining in and breaking off yarns. **Edge stitch:** Worked at each side of armhole steeks and k in background colours on every round. Sts for sleeves are knitted up from edge stitches. **Cross stitch:** With darning needle, overcast raw edge of steek to strands on wrong side of knitting, and after sewing to end, reverse to form cross stitches. See page 137 for full illustrations of steeks, edge stitches, and cross stitch.

BODY
With 3¼mm (US3) needles and D, cast on 320[352] sts. Mark the first st of rnd, and making sure the cast on edge is not twisted, join in and break off colours as required and work the check border as follows:-
Rnd 1: k2 D, k2 R. **Rnd 2:** p2 D, p2 R.
Rnd 3: k2 P, k2 D. **Rnd 4:** p2 P, p2 D.
Rnd 5: k2 D, k2 O. **Rnd 6:** p2 D, p2 O.
Rnd 7: k2 M, k2 K. **Rnd 8:** p2 M, p2 K.
Rnd 9: k2 K, k2 L. **Rnd 10:** p2 K, p2 L.
Rnd 11: k2 J, k2 A. **Rnd 12:** p2 J, p2 A.
Rnd 13: k2 A, k2 I. **Rnd 14:** p2 A, p2 I.
Mark the first st of rnd, and joining in and breaking off colours as required, work the chart patt as follows:-
First Size Only: Rep the 32 patt sts 10 times in the round.
Second Size Only: Beg at 9th st of chart and work the last 24 sts; rep the 32 patt sts 10 times; work the first 8 sts of chart.
Both Sizes: Continue as set and work the first 9 rnds once only, and thereafter, rep rnds 10 through 49. Work 74[76] chart patt rnds from beg. Break off yarns.

Next Rnd – Work Armhole Steeks and Edge Sts
Place the first st of rnd on a safety pin; with colours as for next rnd of chart patt,

CHART A

(chart: 32 pattern sts; rows numbered 1–49)

32 pattern sts

KEY

■	= A	◩	= J
⊥	= B	▼	= K
◪	= C	◿	= L
◉	= D	◇	= M
◎	= E	◆	= N
⊠	= F	∨	= O
⊞	= G	△	= P
☐	= H	◣	= Q
·	= I	◮	= R

cast on 6 sts, in alt colours (the first 5 sts cast on are steek sts, the 6th is the edge st); mark the first st cast on for beg of rnd and centre of first steek; keeping continuity, work the next 159[175] sts in chart patt; place the next st on a safety pin; with alt colours, cast on 12 sts (first and last are edge sts, centre 10 are steek sts); keeping continuity, patt to end of rnd; with alt colours, cast on 6 sts (first st is the edge st, last 5 are steek sts). Work the steek sts in alt colours and the edge sts in darker colour throughout, and keeping continuity, work chart patt on 159[175] sts of back and front. Continue as set until 127[136] chart patt rnds are worked from beg.

Next Rnd – Begin Front Neck Shaping
With colours as for next rnd of chart patt, work 5 steek sts, 1 edge st, and keeping continuity, patt 62[68] sts from chart; place the next 35[39] sts on a holder for front neck; with alt colours, cast on 10 steek sts; continue as set to end of rnd.

Work front neck steek in alt colours, and keeping continuity, dec 1 st at each side of front neck steek on next 7 rnds. Patt 1 rnd straight, then dec at each side of front neck steek on next and every foll alt rnd 3 times. 52[58] chart patt sts rem on front shoulders.

Next Rnd – Begin Back Neck Shaping
With colours as for next rnd of chart, patt straight to 159[175] back patt sts; keeping continuity, patt 52[58] sts; place the next 55[59] sts on a holder for back neck; with alt colours, cast on 10 steek sts; continue as set to end of rnd. Keeping continuity, dec 1 st at each side of front and back neck steeks on next and every foll alt rnd until 49[55] chart patt sts rem on each shoulder. Patt 2 rnds straight, then patt 1 more rnd casting off all steek sts.

With R[J] graft shoulder and edge sts together. See page 137 for grafting. With A, sew backstitch up centre of first and

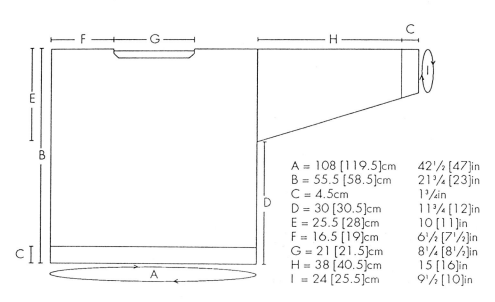

Shrouded in mist and secrecy, evoking memories of ancient legends, the lady of the lake arrives wearing this beautiful Celtic key sweater under her velvet cloak.

A = 108 [119.5]cm   42½ [47]in
B = 55.5 [58.5]cm   21¾ [23]in
C = 4.5cm   1¾in
D = 30 [30.5]cm   11¾ [12]in
E = 25.5 [28]cm   10 [11]in
F = 16.5 [19]cm   6½ [7½]in
G = 21 [21.5]cm   8¼ [8½]in
H = 38 [40.5]cm   15 [16]in
I = 24 [25.5]cm   9½ [10]in

last armhole steek. Cut open armhole steeks up centre between 5th and 6th sts.

SLEEVES

With F, pick up and k the st from safety pin and mark this st for beg of rnd; knit up 151[165] sts evenly around armhole, working into loop of edge st next to chart patt. Beg at rnd 10 of chart and patt sleeve as follows :-
K marked st in darker colour; work the last 11[2] sts of chart; rep the 32 patt sts 4[5] times; work the first 12[3] sts of chart.

Continue as set, repeating rnds 10 through 49, and keeping continuity, dec 1 st at each side of marked st on every 3rd rnd 32[30] times. 88[106] sts rem. Then dec as set on every foll alt rnd until 72[76] sts rem. Work 14 rnds of check border as body, working first size in colours as rnd 14 working back through rnd 1, and second size in colours as rnd 1 through 14. With D[A], cast off knitwise.

NECKBAND

With A, sew backstitch up centre of first and last steek sts. Cut open front and back neck steeks up centre, between 5th and 6th sts. With K, pick up and k the 55[59] sts from back holder, decreasing 1 st at centre; knit up 24 sts to front holder; pick up and k the 35[39] sts from holder, decreasing 1 st at centre; knit up 24 sts to complete rnd. 136[144] sts. Work check border in colours as body from rnd 8 working back through rnd 1. With D, cast off knitwise.

Trim all steeks to 3 sts and cross st in position. Darn in all loose ends. Press lightly on wrong side, omitting check borders.

ALBA
CELTIC KEY
JACKET

RATING
★ ★

SIZES
One size fits bust 86-102cm 34-40in.

KNITTED
MEASUREMENTS
Width underarm (buttoned) 132cm (52in).
Length from top of shoulder 76cm (30in).
Sleeve length 41cm (16¼in).

MATERIALS
Yarn: Rowan Lambswool Tweed; Rowan
DDK; Rowan Kid/Silk; Rowan LDK; Rowan
Wool/Cotton.

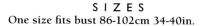

A. Dark Ore Lambswool Tweed (183)
150g; **B.** Pillar Box LDK (45) 50g;
C. Sienna LDK (77) 125g; **D.** Kohl
Lambswool Tweed (185) 100g; **E.** Russet
DDK (663) 100g; **F.** Red Rust DDK (627)
100g; **G.** Bluster Lambswool Tweed (184)
50g; **H.** Garnet Kid Silk (992) 25g;
I. Cinnamon LDK (78) 50g; **J.** Steel Blue
Kid Silk (991) 50g; **K.** Musk Wool/Cotton
(913) 40g; **L.** Blue Grey DDK (65) 50g;
M. Ruby Red DDK (651) 50g; **N.** Crushed
Berry Kid Silk (993) 50g; **O.** Dark Green
DDK (658) 50g; **P.** Rose Pink DDK (70)
50g; **Q.** Potpourri Kid Silk (996) 50g;
R. Dark Emerald Lambswool Tweed (182)
50g; **S.** Dried Rose Silkstones * (825) 25g.

Note: Yarn marked with * is used doubled
throughout.

1 set of double pointed or circular needles
in 3¼mm (US3) and 3¾mm (US5). 3
Stitch holders. 2 Safety pins. Stitch
markers. 12 Buttons.

TENSION (GAUGE)
20 sts and 22 rows to 8cm (18 sts and 21
rows to 3in), measured over chart patt,
using 3 3/4mm (US5) needles and working
the patt on right side only, breaking off the
yarns at the end of every row. See page
137 for making a Fair Isle swatch.

STITCHES
2/2 rib: K2 with first colour, p2 with
second colour, stranding the yarns evenly
across wrong side. **Chart patt:** K every
round, and on two-colour rounds, strand
the yarn not in immediate use evenly
across wrong side. On stretches of more
than 7 sts in one colour, weave in yarn not
in use at centre of stretch. **Steeks:** Worked
at front, armholes, and neck, and later cut
up centre to form openings. The steek is
worked over 10 sts. K these sts on every
round, and on two-colour rounds, k each
st and round in alt colours. Do not weave
in newly joined in or broken off yarns at
centre of front steek. Instead leave approx.
5cm (2in) tail when joining in and
breaking off yarns. **Edge stitch**: Worked at
each side of front and armhole steeks and
k in background colours on every round.
Sts for sleeves and front bands are knitted
up from edge stitches. **Cross stitch**: With
darning needle, overcast raw edge of steek
to strands on wrong side of knitting, and
knitting, and after sewing to end, reverse
to form cross stitches. See page 137 for
full illustrations of steeks, edge sts, and
cross stitch.

BODY
With 3¼mm (US3) needles and A, cast on
306 sts.
Mark the first st of rnd, and making sure
the cast on edge is not twisted, join in B
and work steek, edge sts and 2/2 rib as
follows :-
Rnd 1: With alt colours, k5 steek sts; with
A, k1 edge st; * k2 A, p2 B; rep from * to
the last 8 sts; k2 A, with A, k1 edge st;
with alt colours, k5 steek sts.
Rnd 2: As set, using C instead of B.
Rnds 3 and 4: As set, using D instead of
A.
Rnds 5 and 6: As set, using E instead of
C.
Rnd 7: As set, using F instead of E.
Rnd 8: As set, using G instead of D.
Rnd 9: As set, using H instead of G, and I
instead of F.
Rnd 10: As set, using J instead of H.
Rnd 11: As set, using K instead of I.
Rnd 12: As set, using L instead of J.
Rnds 13 through 23: Working back, as
rnds 11 through 1.

Next Rnd – Increase
With A, k10; * m1, k11; rep from * to last
10 sts; m1, k10. 333 sts. Change to 3¾mm
(US5) needles, mark the first st of rnd, and
using colours as indicated on chart, work
as follows:-
With alt colours, k5 steek sts: with darker
colour, k1 edge st; work patt from chart,
repeating the 32 patt sts 10 times, then

*In this design I have worked the
same pattern using warmer shades
to give a change of mood. This is a
classic, dropped shoulder jacket in
an easy, loose fitting style.*

*'Alba' represents Fair Isle knitting in its
most intricate and fascinating form where
the many colours (19 in this design) used
in the background blend and harmonize
together in patterned bands.*

KEY

- ⊡ = A
- Z = B
- ◈ = C
- ■ = D
- ∕ = E
- ⊥ = F
- ◢ = G
- ∧ = H
- △ = I
- ◆ = J
- ☐ = K
- ✳ = L
- ⊙ = M
- ☒ = N
- ▼ = O
- ⊞ = P
- ⊟ = Q
- ▷ = R
- ▢ = S

CHART A

◀ last st   ◀ 32 pattern sts ▶

To make this jacket, follow the traditional method of knitting Fair Isle designs. Work in one piece on a circular knitting needle.

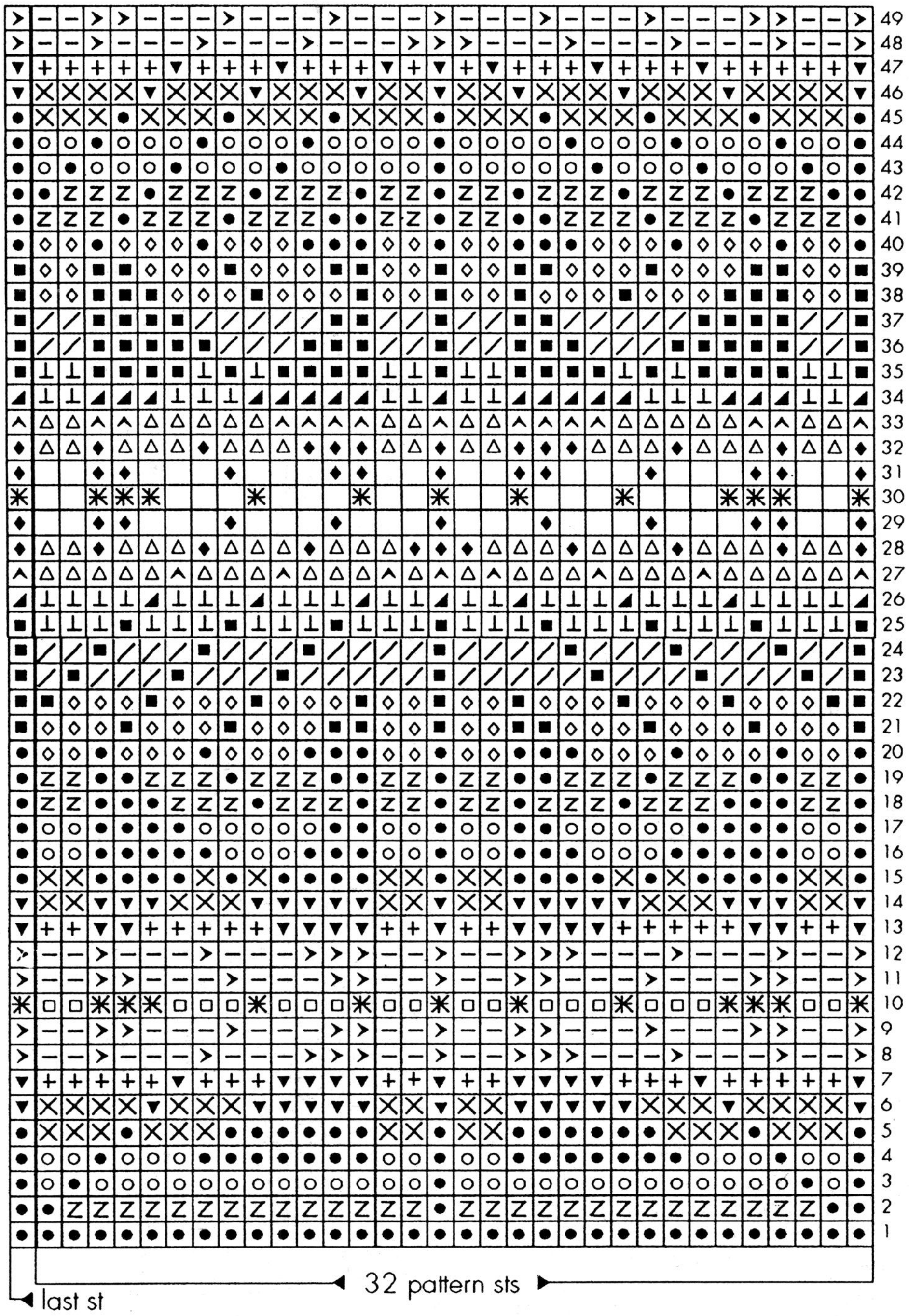

work the last st from chart; with darker colour, k1 edge st; with alt colours, k5 steek sts. Joining in and breaking off colours as required, continue as set, working the first 9 rnds of chart patt once only, and thereafter repeating rnds 10 through 49. Work 106 chart patt rnds.

Next Rnd – Work Armhole Steeks and Edge Sts

With colours as for next rnd of chart patt, and keeping continuity, k5 steek sts; k1 edge st; patt 80 sts; place the next st on a safety pin; with alt colours, cast on 12 sts (first and last are edge sts, centre 10 are steek sts); patt 159 sts of back; place the next st on a safety pin; cast on 12 sts as previously; patt 80 sts; k1 edge st; k5 steek sts.

Continue straight in chart patt and work armhole steeks and edge sts as front until 166 chart patt rnds have been worked.

Next Rnd – Begin Front Neck Shaping

With colours as for next rnd of chart patt and keeping continuity, cast off 5 steek sts; k1 edge st; work as set to the last 5 sts of rnd; with alt colours, cast off last 5 steek sts and break off yarns.

Next Rnd:

Place the first 8 sts of rnd on a holder for right front neck; with colours as for next chart patt rnd, cast on 5 steek sts, marking the first st cast on for beg of rnd; keeping continuity, work to the last 8 sts of rnd and place these sts on a holder for left front neck: with alt colours, cast on 5 steek sts. Continue as set, and keeping continuity of chart patt, dec 1 st at each side of front neck steek on next 12 rnds. Work 1 rnd straight, then work 1 more rnd decreasing at front neck as previously.

Next Rnd – Begin Back Neck Shaping

Keeping continuity, work straight to beg of back neck steek; patt 60 sts; place the next 39 sts on a holder for back neck; with alt colours, cast on 10 steek sts; patt to end of rnd. Continue as set and dec 1 st at each side of front and back neck steeks on next and foll alt rnds twice. 57 chart patt sts rem on each shoulder. Work 2 rnds straight, casting off all steek sts on last rnd. With L, graft shoulder and edge sts together. See page 137 for grafting. Using O with ply split in two, sew backstitch

along first and last armhole steek sts. Cut open armhole steeks up centre between 5th and 6th sts.

SLEEVES

With 3¾mm (US5) needles and R, pick up and k the st from safety pin and mark this st for beg of rnd; knit up 151 sts evenly around armhole, working into loop of edge st next to chart patt.

Joining in and breaking off colours as required, beg at rnd 10 of chart patt and k the marked st in L; patt the last 11 sts of st rep; rep the 32 patt sts 4 times; patt the first 12 sts of chart. Work the marked st in darker colours throughout, and the rem sts in chart patt. Repeat rnds 10 through 49 twice, then work rnds 10 through 20. AT THE SAME TIME, shape sleeve:-
Dec 1 st at each side of marked st on every 3rd rnd 13 times. 126 sts rem. Then on every foll alt rnd 25 times. 76 sts rem.

Next Rnd – Dec for cuff

With A, (k2tog, k2) 8 times; (k2tog, k1) 4 times; (k2tog, k2) 8 times. 56 sts. Change to 3¼mm (US3) needles and work 23 rnds in 2/2 rib in colours as for body. With A, cast off evenly in rib.

The colour detail in the main fabric follows through into the ribbed border where the knit two and purl two stitches are worked in alternating shades.

Sew backstitch along first and last neck and front steek sts as for armholes. Cut open centre front steek between first and last sts of rnd. Cut open front and back neck steeks up centre between 5th and 6th steek sts.

NECKBAND
With right side facing, 3¼mm (US3) needles and J, pick up and k the 8 sts from right front holder; knit up 29 sts evenly to back neck holder; pick up and k the 39 sts from back neck holder and dec 1 st at centre; knit up 29 sts evenly to left neck holder; pick up and k the 8 sts from holder. 112 sts. The first and last sts are edge sts. Working in colours as for rnd 10 back through 1 of body, work 2/2 rib and beg and end wrong side rows with p3 in darker colours, and right side rows with k3 in darker colours.

LEFT FRONT BAND
With right side facing, 3¼mm (US3) needles and J, knit up 170 sts along left front opening, working into edge sts as for sleeves. Work 10 rows 2/2 rib in colours as neckband, beginning and ending wrong side rows with p2 in darker colours, and right side rows with k2 in darker colours.

RIGHT FRONT BAND
As left, with the addition of 12 buttonholes to be worked on 5th row, as follows:-
Rib 4, (cast off 2, rib 12, cast off 2, rib 13) 5 times, cast off 2, rib 12, cast off 2, rib 5.
Next Row: Continue in rib and cast on 2 sts over those cast off.

Trim all steeks to 2 sts and cross st in position. Darn in all loose ends. Sew on buttons to correspond with buttonholes.

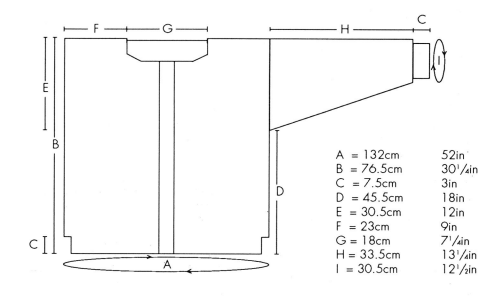

A = 132cm	52in
B = 76.5cm	30¼in
C = 7.5cm	3in
D = 45.5cm	18in
E = 30.5cm	12in
F = 23cm	9in
G = 18cm	7¼in
H = 33.5cm	13¼in
I = 30.5cm	12½in

ABERLADY
CELTIC KEY SWEATER

RATING

★ ★ ★

SIZES
To fit bust 81-84[86-91,94-99]cm
32-33[34-36, 37-39]in.
Directions for larger sizes are given in
parenthesis. Where there is only one set of
figures, it applies to all sizes.

KNITTED MEASUREMENTS
Width around hemline 89[98,106.5]cm
35[38½, 42]in.
Underarm including gussets
101.5[110.5,119.5]cm 40 [43½,47]in.
Length from top of shoulder 52[56,59]cm
20½ [22,23¼] in.
Sleeve length 45[48,51]cm 17¾[18¼,20]in.

MATERIALS
Yarn: Rowan Edina Ronay Silk/Wool.
22[24,26] 20g balls in shade no. 852 Moss
Green.

1 set of double-pointed or circular 2¾mm
(US2) needles. 9 stitch holders. Stitch
markers. 1 Button.

The texture of the raised arrowhead pattern here creates a two-tone effect. Knitted in the traditional seamless manner, with underarm gussets, 'Aberlady' is a neat design with a neck fastening detail.

The arrowhead key pattern, worked in a single colour, proves equally successful as a textured design. Knitted on fine needles in a silk and wool yarn, raised purl stitches against a stocking stitch background produce an effect that is very detailed and luxurious. The style is based on the traditional fisher gansey - close fitting and seamless, with diamond-shaped underarm gussets that is very much in keeping with knitting traditions from the Scottish East Coast.

TENSION (GAUGE)
18 sts and 25 rows to 5cm (2in), measured over chart patt, using 2¾mm (US2) needles.

STITCHES
The pattern is composed of purl sts on a st.st. ground. The underarm gussets are worked in st.st.

BODY
Cast on 320[352,384] sts. Place a marker on first st of rnd, and making sure cast on edge is not twisted, work border as follows: –
Rnds 1 and 2: Purl. **Rnd 3**: Knit. **Rnds 4** and 5: K2, p2. **Rnds 6 and 7**: P2, k2.
Rnds 8 through 15: Rep rnds 4 through 7 twice again. **Rnd 16**: Knit. **Rnds 17 and 18**: Purl. Mark the first st of rnd.

First and third sizes only: Rep the 32 patt sts from chart 10 [12] times in the rnd. **Second size only**: Beg all rnds at 9th st of chart and patt the last 24 sts; rep the 32 patt sts 10 times; patt the first 8 sts of chart. **All sizes**: Mark the centre st (161st, 177th, 193rd st of rnd). Work the first 9 rnds of chart once only, and thereafter rep rnds 10 through 29. Continue as set until piece measures 23[25,26]cm 9 [9¾,10¼]in from beg.

KEY

☐ = k on right side, p on wrong side
◉ = p on right side, k on wrong side

CHART A

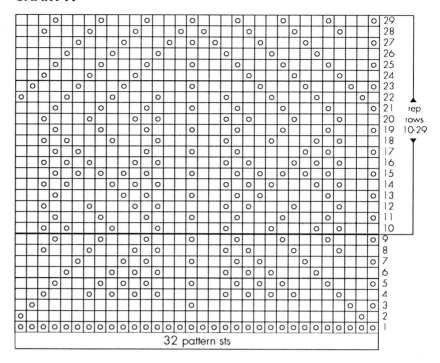

32 pattern sts

rep rows 10-29

Next Rnd – Begin Underarm Gussets
Inc 1 st at each side of first st; keeping continuity, patt to marked centre st and inc 1 st at each side of this st; keeping continuity, patt to end of rnd. Patt as set for the next 3 rnds, working the 3 gusset sts in st.st. (k every rnd). **Next rnd**: * M1, k3 , m1; patt 159[175,191] sts as set; rep from * once again. Continue in this manner, increasing 1 st at each side of gussets on every 4th rnd and working the inc sts in st.st. until there are 25 sts in each gusset. Place the gusset sts on holders, and the first 159[175,191] sts on a spare needle.

Back Armhole
Working back and forth on wrong and right sides, continue in patt as set over the 159[175,191]sts of back until armhole measures 20[22,24]cm 8[8¾,9¼]in. Place the centre 51[55,59] sts on a holder for back neck. Place the rem shoulder sts on holders.

Front Armhole
With right side facing, rejoin yarn and patt 159[175,191] sts of front as set, until armhole measures 12[13,14]cm 4¾[5,5½]in with right side facing for next row.

Left Neck Opening
Row 1: Patt 76[84,92] sts as set; k2, p2, k3; leave rem sts on a spare needle. **Row 2**: K1, p2, k2, p2; patt as set to end. **Row 3**: Patt as set to the last 7 sts; p2, k2, p2, k1. **Row 4**: K3, p2, k2; patt as set to end. Rep the last 4 rows until opening measures 2cm ¾in, with wrong side facing for next row. **Make buttonhole**: K2, cast off 2, continue as set to end. On the next row cast on 2 sts over those cast off. Continue as set until opening measures 3cm 1¼in with wrong side facing for next row. Cast off 7, patt to end.

Shape Left Neck
Row 1: Patt as set to the last 7 sts; place these sts on a holder. **Row 2**: keeping continuity, patt to end. Row 3: Patt as set to the last 2 sts; place these sts on holder. **Row 4**: As row 2. Rep rows 3 and 4 once again. Keeping continuity of patt, dec 1 st at neck edge of next 7[8,8] rows. Patt 1 row straight. Dec 1 st at neck edge of next and every foll alt row until 54[60,66] sts rem. Continue straight in patt until front corresponds in length with back. Place sts on a holder.

Right Neck Opening
Cast on 7 sts, and with right side facing, keep continuity and patt the 76[84,92] sts of right front. Continue in patt as set over the right front sts and work the 7 sts cast on as 7 sts on left opening edge, omitting buttonhole. Continue in this manner until

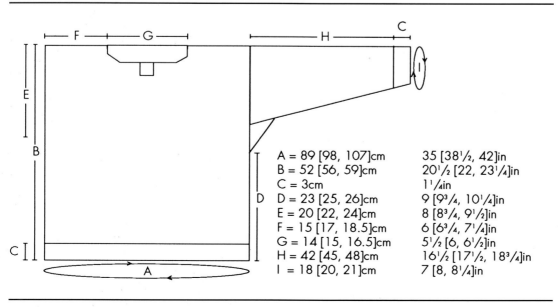

A = 89 [98, 107]cm   35 [38½, 42]in
B = 52 [56, 59]cm   20½ [22, 23¼]in
C = 3cm   1¼in
D = 23 [25, 26]cm   9 [9¾, 10¼]in
E = 20 [22, 24]cm   8 [8¾, 9½]in
F = 15 [17, 18.5]cm   6 [6¾, 7¼]in
G = 14 [15, 16.5]cm   5½ [6, 6½]in
H = 42 [45, 48]cm   16½ [17½, 18¾]in
I = 18 [20, 21]cm   7 [8, 8¼]in

A soft yarn in a mixture of silk and wool produces a luxurious fabric for this formal sweater with its repeating key motifs. A frilled shirt softens the neckline.

opening measures 3cm 1¼in with right side facing for next row. Cast off 8 sts; patt as set to end.

Shape Right Neck – As left neck.

Shoulder Seams
Place back and front shoulder sts on needles and join shoulders by casting off sts together on right side.

SLEEVES

With right side facing, pick up and k the 25 gusset sts; knit up 145[159,173] sts evenly around armhole. **Next rnd**: Ssk, k21, k2tog; working from rnd 10, patt the last 8[15,11] sts of chart patt; rep the 32 patt sts 4[4,5] times, patt the last 9[16,12] sts of chart. Continue sleeve patt as set, repeating rnds 10 through 29, and work the gusset sts in st.st. decreasing 1 st at each side of gusset on every 4th rnd until 1 gusset st remains. Keeping continuity of patt, dec 1 st at each side of gusset st on every foll 4th rnd until 64[70,76] sts rem. Patt straight until sleeve measures 42[45,48]cm 16½[17½, 18¾]in. Work rnds 1 through 18 of body border. Cast off knitwise.

COLLAR

With right side facing, pick up and k the 11 sts from left front neck; knit up 15[19,21] sts to back neck holder; pick up and k the 51[55,59] sts from holder and dec 1 st at centre; knit up 15[9,21] sts to right front holder; pick up and k the 11 sts from holder. 102[114,126] sts. Working back and forth, k1, p1 rib for 4[6,8] rows. Begin with right side facing, and work as follows:-
Row 1: * K2, p2; rep from * to last 2sts; k2.
Rows 2 and 3: * P2, k2; rep from * to last 2 sts; p2.
Row 4: As row 1. Rep rows 1–4 3 more times. K 1 row. P 2 rows. Cast off knitwise.

Sew on button to correspond with buttonhole. Do not press garment.

'Aberlady' dominates a landscape in the many shades of green that Ireland is renowned for.

ROSEMARKIE
CELTIC KEY
WAISTCOAT

RATING

★

SIZES
To fit chest/bust 86-91[97-102,104-109]cm 34-36[38-40, 41-43]in.
Directions for larger sizes are given in parenthesis. Where there is only one set of figures, it applies to all sizes.

KNITTED MEASUREMENTS
Underarm (buttoned) 103[112,119]cm 41[44,46¾]in.
Length from top of shoulder 57[60,62]cm 22½[23½, 24½]in.

MATERIALS
Yarn: Rowan Donegal Lambswool Tweed; Fine Cotton Chenille.

A. Rye Donegal Tweed (474) 150[150,175]g; **B.** Cinnamon Donegal Tweed (479) 50[75,75]g; **C.** Oak Fine Chenille (397) 50g; **D.** Lacquer Fine Chenille (388) 50[75,75]g; **E.** Roseberry Donegal Tweed (480) 50g; **F.** Cyclamen Fine Chenille (385) 50g.

1 set of 4 double-pointed, or circular 2¾mm (US2) and 3¼mm (US3) needles. 3 Stitch holders. Stitch markers. Darning needle. 7[7,8] buttons.

In a very romantic mood on the misty moorlands.

Another Pictish Celtic stone from North Eastern Scotland, the Rosemarkie stone, is the source of this key pattern. I have used it for a classic waistcoat that is an ideal introductory project to the Fair Isle technique. Unlike some of my other patterns which use many colours, this design is very easy to work in a simple, but effective, scheme of six warm rosy colours on a light tweedy background.

TENSION (GAUGE)
31 sts and 36 rows to 10cm (4in), measured over patt, using 3¼mm (US3) needles, and working the patt on right side only, breaking off yarns at the end of every row. See page 137 for working a Fair Isle swatch.

STITCHES
2/2 rib: K2 with the first colour, p2 with second colour, stranding the yarns evenly across wrong side. **Chart patt**: K every round , and on two-colour rounds, strand the yarn not in immediate use evenly across wrong side. **Steeks**: Worked at front, armholes, and neck, and later cut up centre to form openings. The steek is worked over 10 sts. K these sts on every round, and on two-colour rounds, k each st and round in alternating colours. Do not weave in newly joined or broken off yarns at centre of front steek. Instead leave approx. 5cm (2in) tail when joining in and breaking off yarns. **Edge stitch**: Worked at each side of front and armhole steeks and k in background colour on every round. Sts for front bands are knitted up from edge sts. **Cross stitch**: With darning needle, overcast raw edge of steek to strands on wrong side of knitting, and after sewing to end, reverse to form cross stitches. See page 137 for full illustrations on steeks, edge sts and cross stitch.

CHART A

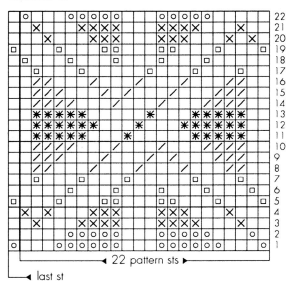

◄— 22 pattern sts —►

└— ◄ last st

KEY

□	= A
⊡	= B
☒	= C
⊡	= D
⧄	= E
⊠	= F

137[147,155] sts; place the next 17[19,21] sts on a holder; with alt colours, cast on 10 steek sts; keeping continuity of chart, patt 67[71,76] sts; k2tog; k1 edge st and mark it; k5 steek sts.

Keeping continuity of chart patt, and working all steeks in alt colours, dec 1 st at each side of front steek as set on every 3rd rnd, and dec 1 st at each side of armhole steeks on next 7[8,9] rnds and then on foll 7[8,8] alt rnds. 109[115,121] chart patt sts rem across back.

Keeping continuity of chart, work straight at armholes and continue to dec at front on every 3rd rnd, until body measures 21.5[23,24]cm 8½[9,9½]in from beg of armhole shaping.

Shape Back Neck
Continue to dec at front as set, and keeping continuity of chart, work straight to 109[115,121] patt sts of back; patt 31[32,34] sts; place the next 47[51,53] sts on a holder; with alt colours, cast on 10 steek sts; keeping continuity of chart, work as set to end of rnd.

B O D Y
With 2¾mm (US2) needles and A, cast on 302[322,342]sts. Mark the first st of rnd, and making sure that cast on edge is not twisted, join in B and work 2/2 rib as follows:-
Rnds 1 and 2: With alt colours, k5 steek sts; k edge st with A; * k2 A, p2 B; rep from * to the last 8 sts; k2 A; k1 edge st with A ; with alt colours, k5 steek sts.
Rnds 3 and 4: As rnds 1 and 2 but substituting C for B. **Rnds 5 and 6**: As rnds 1 and 2 but substituting D for C.
Rnds 7 and 8: As rnds 1 and 2 but substituting E for D. **Rnds 9 and 10**: As rnds 1 and 2 but substituting F for E.
Rnds 11 and 12: As rnds 7 and 8. **Rnds 13 and 14**: As rnds 5 and 6. **Rnds 15 and 16**: As rnds 3 and 4. **Rnds 17 and 18**: As rnds 1 and 2. **Rnds 19 through 24**: As rnds 3 through 8.

Next rnd – Increase
With A, k5 steek sts; k1 edge st; k1[5,0]; * m1, k16[15,15]; rep from * to the last 7[11,6] sts; m1, k1[5,0]; k1 edge st; k5 steek sts. 321[343,365] sts.

Change to 3¼mm (US3) needles, and joining in and breaking off colours as required, work steeks, edge sts and chart patt as follows:-
With colours as rnd 1 of chart, k5 steek sts with alt colours; k1 edge st with A; rep the 22 chart patt sts 14[15,16] times; work the last st of chart; k1 edge st with A; k5 steek sts with alt colours. Working rnd 2 on

chart patt sts, mark centre underarm sts on next rnd as follows:-
K5 steek sts; k1 edge st; patt 77[82,88] sts; patt the next st and mark it; patt 153[165,175] sts; patt the next st and mark it; patt 77[82,88] sts; k1 edge st; k5 steek sts. Continue as set and rep the 22 patt rnds until body measures 33[34.5,35.5]cm 13[13½,14]in from beg.

Shape Armholes and V-neck
With colours as for next rnd of chart, k5 steek sts; k1 edge st and mark it; ssk; keeping continuity of chart, patt 67[71,76] sts; place the next 17[19,21] sts on a holder; with alt colours, cast on 10 steek sts; keeping continuity of chart, patt

Previous page: Styled in a traditional manner the rich colours used here are a perfect accompaniment for the deep hues of velvet skirts and the burnished wood of a violin.

A = 103 [112, 119]cm
B = 57 [60, 62]cm
C = 6cm
D = 24 [25.5, 26.5]cm
E = 33 [34.5, 35.5]cm
F = 9 [9.25, 10]cm
G = 18 [19, 19.5]cm

A = 41 [44, 46¾]in
B = 22½ [23½, 24½]in
C = 2½in
D = 9½ [10, 10½]in
E = 13 [13½, 14]in
F = 3½ [3¾, 4]in
G = 7 [7½, 7¾]in

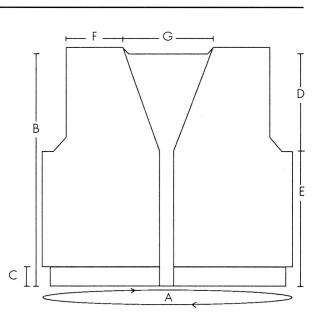

From a distance the lighter shades of the key pattern are strikingly apparent against a darker background.

Keeping continuity of chart, continue to dec at front as set until 28[29,31] patt sts rem on front shoulders, and dec 1 st at each side of back neck steek on next and foll 2 alt rnds. 28[29,31] chart patt sts rem on back shoulders. Continue straight as set until body measures 24[25.5,26.5]cm 9½[10,10½]in from beg of armhole shaping. Keeping continuity of chart, patt 1 more rnd casting off all steek sts on this rnd.

With A, graft front and back shoulder and edge sts together. See page 137 for grafting. With A, sew backstitch up centre of first and last armhole steek sts. Cut open armhole steeks up centre, between 5th and 6th sts.

ARMHOLE BANDS

With 2¾mm (US2) needles and A, beg at centre st on holder, and pick up and k9[10,11] sts from holder; knit up 135[141,151] sts evenly around armhole; pick up and k the rem 8[9,10] sts from holder. 152[160,172] sts. Work 10 rnds of 2/2 rib in colours as rnds 9 through 18 of body rib. With A, cast off knitwise.

FRONT BAND

Sew backstitch up centre of first and last sts of front and back steeks. Cut open both steeks up centre, between 5th and 6th sts. With 2¾mm (US2) needles and A, beg at bottom right front and knit up 94[98,102] sts to front neck marker; knit up 76[80,83] sts to back neck holder; pick up and k the 47[51,53] sts from holder, decreasing 1 st at centre; knit up 76[80,83] sts to front neck marker; knit up 94[98,102] sts to bottom left front. 386[406,422] sts. Work 10 rows of 2/2 rib in colours as armhole bands, beg and ending wrong side rows with p2 A, and right side rows with k2 A. Make buttonholes on 5th row for men and 6th row for women as follows:-
Rib 2; * cast off 2, rib 13[13,12]; rep from * 6[6,7] times in all, cast off 2; rib to end of row. On next row, cast on 2 sts over those cast off. After 10 rows, cast off purlwise with A.

FINISHING

Trim all steeks to 3 sts and cross st in position. Press lightly on wrong side, omitting all ribs. Sew on buttons.

LISMORE
CELTIC KEY
SWEATER

RATING

★ ★ ★

SIZES
One size fits chest/bust 86-101cm 34-40in.

KNITTED MEASUREMENTS
Underarm 120cm 47½in.
Length from top of shoulder 63.5cm 24¾in.
Sleeve length 45.5cm 18in.

MATERIALS
Yarn: Rowan Lambswool Tweed; Rowan DDK; Rowan LDK; Rowan Kid/Silk.

A. Petrol LDK (54) 150g; **B.** Old Gold Kid/Silk (989) 75g; **C.** Blue Grey DDK (65) 50g; **D.** Olive DDK (407) 100g; **E.** Dark Ore Lambswool Tweed (183) 100g; **F.** Indigo LDK (108) 25g; **G.** Sea Blue LDK (53) 50g; **H.** Deep Purple DDK (99) 50g; **I.** Steel Blue LDK (52) 25g; **J.** Airforce LDK (88) 100g; **K.** Kohl Lambswool Tweed (185) 50g; **L.** Grey DDK (61) 100g; **M.** Steel Blue Kid/Silk (991) 75g; **N.** Gold LDK (405) 50g; **O.** Red Rust DDK (627) 50g; **P.** Russet DDK (663) 50g; **Q.** Dark Emerald DDK (658) 100g; **R.** Sienna DDK (77) 100g; **S.** Dark Emerald Lambswool Tweed (182) 50g; **T.** Rust DDK (662) 50g.

1 set of double-pointed or circular needles in 3¼mm (US3) and 3¾mm (US5). 4 Stitch holders. Stitch markers.

TENSION (GAUGE)
20 sts and 22 rows to 8cm (19 sts and 21 rows to 3in), measured over chart patt, using 3¾mm (US5) needles and working the patt on the right side only, breaking off yarns at the end of every row. See page 137 for making a Fair Isle swatch.

The moss and heathery tones of the many shades of yarn used in this design blend with, yet define an intricate pattern.

Key patterns were often used to frame a motif on stonework, or the page of a manuscript. Here I chose a stylized flower as the motif and then framed it with a narrow border of the key pattern. Repeating the pattern produced an exotic tiled effect. I wanted to evoke a mood of ancient mystery, so I introduced the deep, subtle colours.

STITCHES
2/2 rib: K2 with first colour, p2 with second colour, stranding the yarn across the wrong side. **Chart patt**: K every round, and on two-colour rounds, strand the yarn not in immediate use evenly across wrong side. On stretches of more than 7 sts in one colour, weave in the yarn not in use on approx every 4th st. **Steeks**: Worked at armholes and front neck, and later cut up centre to form openings. The steek is worked over 10 sts. K these sts on every round, and on two-colour rounds, k each st and round in alt colours. Do not weave in newly joined in or broken off yarns at centre of first armhole steek. Instead leave approx 5cm (2in) tail when joining in and breaking off yarns. **Edge stitch**: Worked at each side of armhole steeks and k in darker colours on every round. Sts for sleeves are knitted up from edge stitches. **Cross stitch**: With darning needle, overcast raw edge of steek to strands on wrong side of knitting, and after sewing to end, reverse to form cross sts. See page 137 for full illustrations of steeks, edge stitches, and cross stitch.

CHART A

KEY

◉ = A
◎ = B
◆ = C
✳ = D
◼ = E
╱ = F
△ = G
Λ = H
◇ = I
⊥ = J
◢ = K
Ƶ = L
+ = M
☒ = N
▢ = O
⬚ = P
▼ = Q
— = R
▷ = S
▫ = T

50 pattern sts

(chart rows numbered 1 through 50)

An original stone cross makes an appropriate backdrop for an up-to-date interpretation of Celtic art.

BODY

With 3¼mm (US3) needles and M, cast on 276 sts. Mark the first st of rnd, and making sure the cast on edge is not twisted, work 2/2 rib as follows:-
Rnd 1: K2 M, p2 N. **Rnd 2**: K2 M, p2 B.
Rnd 3: K2 A, p2 B. **Rnd 4**: K2 A, p2 O.
Rnd 5: K2 Q, p2 O. **Rnds 6 and 7**: K2 Q, p2 P. **Rnd 8**: K2 Q, p2 R. **Rnd 9**: K2 S, p2 R. **Rnd 10**: K2 S, p2 T. **Rnds 11 through 20**: Working back, as rnds 10 through 1.

Next Rnd – Increase: With A, (m1, k12, m1, k13) rep to end of rnd. 300 sts.

Change to 3¾mm (US5) needles, mark first st of rnd, and joining in and breaking off colours as required, work chart patt, repeating the 50 patt sts 6 times in the rnd. Patt the 50 rnds of chart, then work rnds 1 through 30 again. Break off yarns.

Shape Armholes

Place the last 2 sts and first 2 sts of rnd on a holder; with colours as for next rnd of chart patt, cast on 6 sts in alt colours (the first 5 sts cast on are steek sts, the last st cast on is an edge st); mark the first st cast on for beg of rnd; keeping continuity, patt as set over the next 146 sts (front); place the next 4 sts on a holder and with alt colours, cast on 12 sts (the first and last sts cast on are edge sts, the centre 10 sts are steek sts); keeping continuity, patt as set over the rem 146 sts (back): with alt colours, cast on 6 sts (first st cast on is an edge st, the last 5 are steek sts).

Next rnd: (K1 P, k1 Q) 3 times; with Q, ssk; keeping continuity, patt as set over next 142 sts; with Q, k2tog; kl Q, (k1 Q, k1 P) 5 times, kl Q; with Q, ssk; keeping continuity patt as set over the next 142 sts; with Q, k2tog; k2 Q, (k1 P, k1 Q) twice.

Next rnd: (K1 Q, k1 P) twice, k2 Q; continue in chart patt as set over the next 144 sts; k2 Q, (k1 P, k1 Q) 5 times; continue in patt as set over next 144 sts; (k1 Q, k1 P) 3 times.

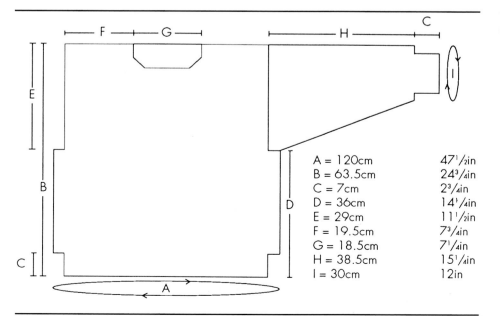

The subtle colouring of 'Lismore' blends with the beauty of the scenery.

A = 120cm	47¹⁄₂in
B = 63.5cm	24³⁄₄in
C = 7cm	2³⁄₄in
D = 36cm	14¹⁄₄in
E = 29cm	11¹⁄₂in
F = 19.5cm	7³⁄₄in
G = 18.5cm	7¹⁄₄in
H = 38.5cm	15¹⁄₄in
I = 30cm	12in

Joining in and breaking off colours as required, continue as set, working steek sts in alt colours on every st and rnd, and edge sts in darker colours. Continue chart patt as set over the 144 sts of front and back until 137 chart patt rnds have been worked from beg.

Shape Front Neck

Work steek and edge sts as set; patt 58 sts as set; place the next 28 sts on a holder; with alt colours, cast on 10 sts for front neck steek; keeping continuity, patt 58 sts; work the rem sts of rnd as set. Work the 10 sts of front neck steek as armhole steeks, and keeping continuity of patt, dec 1 st at each side of front neck steek on next 6 rnds. Work 1 rnd straight, then dec as before, on next and every foll alt rnd 3 times in all (49 chart patt sts rem on each front shoulder). Continue straight for 4 rnds, then work 1 more rnd casting off all steek sts on this rnd. Place the centre 46 sts of back on a holder for back neck. With A, graft shoulder and edge sts together. See page 137 for grafting. With A, sew

backstitch up centre of first and last armhole steek sts. Cut open armhole steeks up centre between 5th and 6th sts.

SLEEVES

With 3¾mm (US5) needles and A, pick up and k the 2 sts on the left side of underarm holder; knit up 147 sts evenly around armhole, working into loop of edge st next to chart patt; pick up and k the rem 2 sts from holder. 151 sts. Place a marker on first st. Joining in and breaking off colours as required, work the marked st in darker colours and work the chart patt over the rem sts, repeating the 50 patt sts 3 times in the rnd. Patt 2 rnds. Keeping continuity of patt, dec 1 st at each side of marked st on next and every foll 3rd rnd 30 times in all (91 sts rem). Then continue to dec as before on every foll alt rnd 8 times (75 sts rem).

Next rnd – Decrease: With A, k1, k2tog; * k2, k2tog; rep from * to end of rnd. 56 sts.

Change to 3¼mm (US3) needles and work 2/2 rib as body for 20 rnds. With M, cast off knitwise.

COLLAR

With A, sew backstitch up centre of first and last steek sts. Cut open steek up centre. With wrong side of garment out, 3¼mm (US3) needles and A, pick up and p the 46 sts from back neck holder; p up 17 sts to front holder; pick up and p the 28 sts from holder; p up 17 sts to form rnd. 108 sts.

Change to 3¾mm (US5) needles and work 2/2 rib for 50 rnds in colour sequence as in chart patt, from rnd 2 through 5, then rnd 8 through 49, then rnd 2 through 5 again. Use the darker colours for k2 and the brighter colours for p2 throughout. With A, cast off knitwise.

FINISHING

Trim steeks to a 2 st width and cross st in position. Darn in all loose ends. Press lightly on wrong side, omitting all ribs.

LINDISFARNE
CELTIC KEY SWEATER

RATING

★ ★ ★

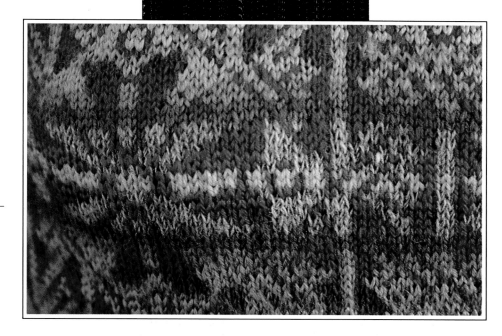

SIZES
One size fits chest/bust 86-97cm 34-38in.

KNITTED MEASUREMENTS
Underarm 112cm 44in.
Length from top of shoulder 63.5cm 25in.
Sleeve length 48cm 19in.

MATERIALS
Yarn: Rowan DDK; Rowan LDK; Rowan Donegal Tweed; Rowan Kid/Silk; Rowan Silk/Wool; Rowan Wool/Cotton; Rowan Silkstones.

A. Sea Green DDK (665) 100g;
B. Roseberry Donegal Tweed (480) 100g;
C. Mauve DDK (118) 50g; **D.** Ruby Red DDK (651) 50g; **E.** Donkey Silk/Wool * (856) 120g; **F.** Sienna LDK (77) 150g;
G. Blue Mist Silkstones (832) 100g;
H. Russet DDK (663) 100g; **I.** Ice Blue LDK (48) 75g; **J.** Blue DDK (672) 50g;
K. Raspberry LDK (601) 75g; **L.** Lavender DDK (666) 50g; **M.** Kashmir Wool/Cotton (910) 40g; **N.** Silver Blonde Kid/Silk (995) 50g.

1 Set of double-pointed or circular needles in 3½mm (US4) and 3¾mm (US5). 2 Safety pins. 2 Stitch holders. Stitch markers. Darning needle.
Note: yarn marked with * is used double throughout.

This sweater displays another basic key pattern from the Rosemarkie stone that is also very similar to those used in the Books of Lindisfarne and Kells. I have elaborated on the original design by inserting large diamond shapes containing a cross motif and based the colours on the beautiful blues and reds found in the Book of Lindisfarne.

The low round neckline of 'Lindisfarne' reflects the design of the main fabric.

TENSION (GAUGE)
12 sts and 14 rows to 5cm (2in) measured over chart patt, using 3¾mm (US5) needles and working on right side only, breaking off yarns at the end of every row. See page 137 for making a Fair Isle swatch.

STITCHES
Chart patt: K every round, and on two-colour rounds, strand the yarn not in immediate use evenly across wrong side. On stretches of more than 7 sts in one colour, weave in the yarn not in use on approx every 4th st. **Steeks**: Worked at armholes and front and back neck, and later cut up centre to form openings. The steek is worked over 10 sts. K these sts on every round, and on two-colour rounds, k each st and round in alt colours. Do not weave in newly joined in or broken off yarns at the centre of the first armhole steek. Instead, leave approx 5cm (2in) tail when joining in and breaking off yarns. **Edge st**: Worked at each side of armhole steeks and k in lighter colours on every round. Sts for sleeves are knitted up from edge sts. **Cross stitch**: With darning needle, overcast raw edge of steek to strands on wrong side of knitting, and after sewing to end, reverse to form cross sts. See page 137 for full illustrations of how to work steeks, edge stitches, and cross stitch.

CHART B

CHART A

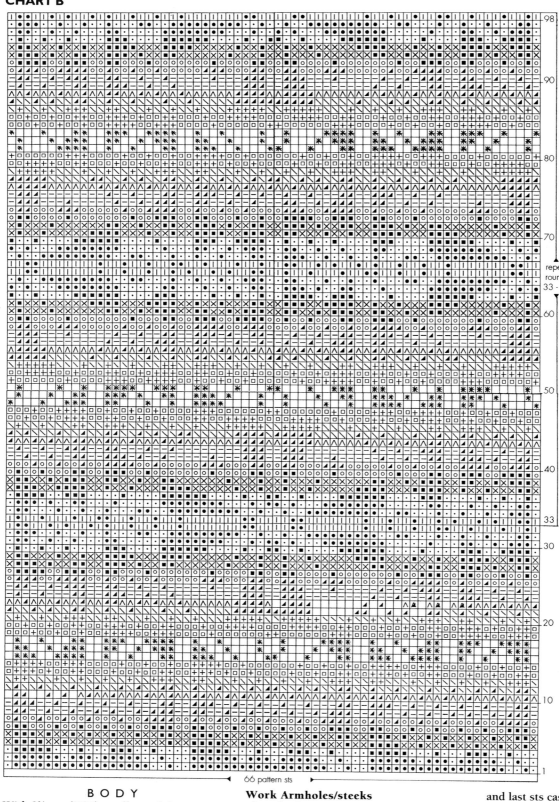

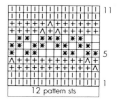

12 pattern sts

repeat rounds 33 - 98

66 pattern sts

KEY

⊞ = A
⊞ = B
⋏ = C
✳ = D
☐ = E
● = F
• = G
■ = H
☒ = I
◎ = J
◢ = K
⊟ = L
◩ = M
▣ = N

Previous page: The rolling countryside, tinted with the mellow shades of setting sunlight is a spectacular backdrop for 'Lindisfarne'.

The setting sun illuminates the colours and patterns in this beautiful knitted sweater making it very reminiscent of the ancient manuscripts.

B O D Y

With 3¾mm (US5) needles and A, cast on 264 sts. Mark the first st of rnd and make sure cast on edge is not twisted. Joining in and breaking off colours as required, work the 11 rnds of chart A, repeating the 12 patt sts 22 times in the rnd. Then joining in and breaking off colours as required, work the 98 rnds of patt from chart B, repeating the 66 patt sts 4 times in the rnd. Break off yarns.

Work Armholes/steeks

Place the first and last st of rnd on a safety pin. Using colours as for rnd 33 of chart B, cast on 6 sts in alternating colours, and mark the first st cast on for beg of rnd (the first 5 sts cast on are steek sts, the last cast on is an edge st); keeping continuity – i.e. beg on 2nd st of chart, work the patt from rnd 33 of chart B and patt 130 sts (front); place the next 2 sts on a safety pin, and with alt colours, cast on 12 sts (the first

and last sts cast on are edge sts, the centre 10 sts are steek sts); keeping continuity patt from chart B as set over the rem 130 sts (back); with alt colours, cast on 6 sts (first st cast on is an edge st, the last 5 sts are steek sts).

Work the steek sts in alt colours, the edge sts in lighter colours, and continue in chart B patt over the 130 sts of front and back, to rnd 78 inclusive.

Surrounded by the stone ruins of Celtic culture, 'Lindisfarne' is a sweater that will look special in any setting. Knitted in the true Fair Isle style, it is a work of art.

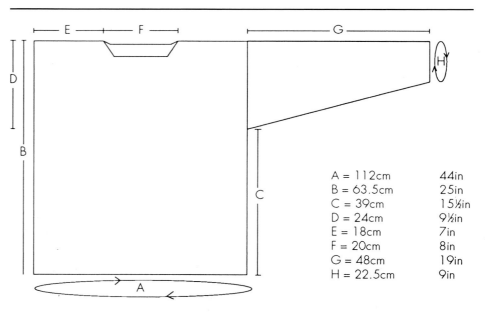

A = 112cm   44in
B = 63.5cm   25in
C = 39cm   15½in
D = 24cm   9½in
E = 18cm   7in
F = 20cm   8in
G = 48cm   19in
H = 22.5cm   9in

Colours and light combine to give a mysterious quality to this beautiful pose.

last sts of rnd and work both these sts in lighter colours throughout. Work chart patt on rem sts as follows:-
Beg at rnd 44 of chart B and work the last 24 sts of chart; work the 66 patt sts once; work the first 24 sts of chart. Continue as set to rnd 46 inclusive.

Next Rnd – Decrease
With colours as for next rnd of chart, k the first st in lighter colour as set; K2tog; keeping continuity, patt to the last 3 sts; ssk; k1 in lighter colour. Keeping continuity, patt 4 rnds straight. Rep these last 5 rnds until 100 sts remain. Then keeping continuity, dec as set on every foll 4th rnd. When chart is worked to rnd 98 inclusive, work from rnd 33 to rnd 98 inclusive once more (60 sts rem). Then work the 11 rnds of chart A, and continue to dec on every 4th rnd as set, until 54 sts remain. With A, p 1 rnd. Change to 3½mm (US4) needles and k 12 rnds. Darn in loose ends on sleeve border. Turn down hem on wrong side at purl rnd, and with darning needle, for hem oversew each stitch to strands on wrong side.

NECKBAND
With A, sew backstitch up centre of first and last sts of front and back neck steeks. Cut steeks open up centre. With 3¼mm (US5) needles and A, pick up and k 42 sts from back neck holder; knit up 19 sts to front neck holder; pick up and k the 28 sts from holder; knit up 19 sts to complete rnd. 108 sts. Mark first st of rnd. Joining in and breaking off colours as required, work the 11 rnds of patt from chart A. With A, p 1 rnd. Change to 3½mm (US4) needles and k 12 rnds. Darn in loose ends on neckband. Turn down hem on wrong side and stitch down as for cuffs.

Body Hem
With right side facing, 3½mm (US4) needles and A, beg at first st of rnd and knit up 1 st into each purl ridge immediately behind cast on edge. 264 sts. K 12 rnds. Darn in loose ends on border and stitch down hem as for cuffs.

FINISHING
Darn in all rem loose ends. Trim all steeks to 2 st width and with A cross st in position. Press lightly on wrong side.

Shape Front Neck
Using colours as for rnd 79 of chart B, patt 5 steek and 1 edge st as set, and continue in chart patt over the next 51 sts; place the next 28 sts on a holder, and with alt colours cast on 10 neck steek sts; keeping continuity, patt the next 51 sts and continue as set to end of rnd. Work steeks, edge sts and back patt as set, and keeping continuity of chart patt, dec 1 st at each side of front neck steek on next 5 rnds. Keeping continuity, patt 1 rnd straight as set, then dec 1 st at each side of front neck steek on next and every foll alt rnd 3 times in all.

Shape Back Neck
Keeping continuity, patt straight as set to back sts; patt 44 sts of back; place the next 42 sts on a holder; with alt colours cast on 10 back neck steek sts; keeping continuity, patt to end of rnd.

Work steeks and edge sts as set, and keeping continuity of chart patt on back and front, dec 1 st at each side of front and back neck steeks on next and foll alt rnd. Patt 1 rnd straight as set, then dec 1 st at each side of back neck steek on next rnd (41 chart patt sts rem on each shoulder). Patt 1 rnd straight as set, then patt final rnd of chart, casting off all steek sts on this rnd.

With A, graft shoulder and edge sts together. See page 137 for grafting. With A, sew backstitch up centre of first and last armhole steek sts. Cut open armhole steeks up centre, between 5th and 6th sts.

SLEEVES
With A, pick up and k the st on the left on safety pin; knit up 114 sts evenly around armhole, working into loop of edge st next to chart patt; pick up and k the rem st from safety pin. Place markers on first and

CELTIC
FRETWORK
PATTERNS

ARDAGH
SWEATER
IN CELTIC FRETWORK

RATING

★ ★

SIZES
To fit chest/bust 81-86 [91-102,107-117]cm
32-34[36-40, 42-46]in.
Directions for larger sizes are given in
parenthesis. Where there is only one set of
figures, it applies to all sizes.

KNITTED MEASUREMENTS
Underarm 106[116,127]cm
41½[45½,50]in.
Length from top of shoulder 61[64,68]cm
24[25¼,26¾]in.
Sleeve seam 46[48,49]cm 18[18¾,19¼]in.

MATERIALS
Yarn: Rowan Donegal Lambswool Tweed;
Fine Cotton Chenille; Silkstones.

A. Sapphire Donegal Tweed (486)
200[225,250]g; **B.** Blue Mist Silkstones
(832) 75g; **C.** Mole Fine Chenille (380)
100g; **D.** Privet Fine Chenille (394) 50g;
E. Dragonfly Silkstones (823) 75g;
F. Marble Silkstones (833) 75g;
G. Eau de Nil Silkstones (835) 75g;
H. Turquoise Fine Chenille (383) 100g;
I. Maple Fine Chenille (396) 50g.

1 Pair each 2¾mm (US2) and 3¼mm (US3)
needles. 1 set of double-pointed or 40cm
(16in) circular 2¾mm (US2) needles. 2
Stitch holders. Stitch markers. Darning
needle.

TENSION (GAUGE)
29 sts and 33 rows to 10cm (4in),
measured over chart pattern, using 3¼mm
(US3) needles.

STITCHES
2/2 rib: K2 with first colour, p2 with
second colour, stranding the yarns evenly
across the wrong side. **Chart patt**: Worked
entirely in st.st. beg with a k row. Odd
numbered rows are right side, even are

*The geometric precision of this design is
very appealing. Although the diamond
shapes and grids have a graphic outline, the
effect is softened by combining soft tweeds
with luxurious silk and chenille yarns.*

*The Ardagh Chalice is an astonishingly fine piece of Celtic art from the first
millennnium A.D. that is now in the National Museum of Ireland in Dublin. I
was intrigued by the ornamental fretwork patterns on the glass studs which
decorate it, and used them as the basis of this design. The diamond-shaped
grid on this sweater is coloured with a mixture of soft and striking blues that
resembles a work of art in stained glass.*

wrong side. Yarn A is carried across all
rows. Use separate lengths of yarn for each
contrast colour area. Approx. 92cm (36in)
lengths of B and F; 81cm (32in) of C and
E; 64cm (25in) of G and H; 46cm (18in) of
D; 38cm (15in) of I, will be sufficient to
knit each separate area of colour, with
enough to weave in or darn in at beg and
end. Before working each contrast area,
wrap the contrast yarn around A on every
row to avoid gaps. See page 137 for
intarsia knitting.

BACK
With 2¾mm (US2) needles and A, cast on
132[144,156] sts. Joining in and breaking
off colours as required, work 2/2 rib as
follows:-
Row 1: K2 A, p2 C. **Row 2**: K2 C, p2 A.

Row 3: K2 A, p2 E. **Row 4**: K2 E, p2 A.
Row 5: K2 A, p2 G. **Row 6**: K2 G, p2 A.
Row 7: K2 A, p2 H. **Row 8**: K2 H, p2 A.
Rep this sequence until rib measures 6.5
[7,7]cm 2½[2¾,2¾]in, with wrong side
facing for next row.

Next row – Increase: With A, p3 [2,6],
* m1, p7 [7,6]; rep from * to the last
3[2,6] sts; m1, k3[2,6]. 151[165,181] sts.

Change to 3¼mm (US3) needles and,
joining in and breaking off colours as
required, work the patt from chart,
repeating the 30 patt sts 5[5,6] times, and
working the first 0[7,0] sts and the last
1[8,1] sts on right side rows, and the first
1[8,1] sts and the last 0[7,0] sts on wrong
side rows, as indicated on chart.

CHART A

KEY

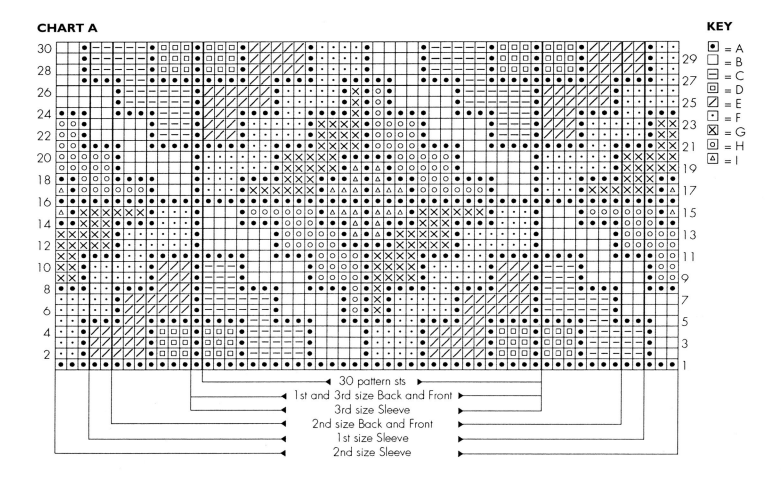

◉ = A	▣ = D	⊡ = G
□ = B	⟋ = E	⊡ = H
⊟ = C	• = F	◭ = I

◄ 30 pattern sts ►
◄ 1st and 3rd size Back and Front ►
◄ 3rd size Sleeve ►
◄ 2nd size Back and Front ►
◄ 1st size Sleeve ►
◄ 2nd size Sleeve ►

Continue straight as set, repeating the 30 patt rows until back measures 61[64,68]cm 24[25¼,26¾]in, with right side facing for next row.

Shape Shoulders and Neck
With A, cast off 16[18,20] sts; keeping continuity, patt the next 36[39,44] sts, including st already on needle; place the

next 47[51,53] sts on a holder; turn, and keeping continuity of patt, work the first set of sts for right shoulder, as follows:-
Row 1: With A, cast off 2 sts, patt to end. **Row 2**: With A, cast off 16[18,20] sts, patt to end. **Row 3**: P2tog, patt to end. With A, cast off rem 17[18,21] sts.

With right side facing, rejoin A and, keeping continuity, patt the rem 52[57,64]

sts of left shoulder, then shape as follows:-
Row 1: With wrong side facing and A, cast off 16[18,20] sts, patt to end. **Row 2**: Cast off 2 sts, patt to end. **Row 3**: Cast off 16[18,20] sts, patt to end. **Row 4**: K2tog, patt to end. With A, cast off the rem 17[18,21] sts.

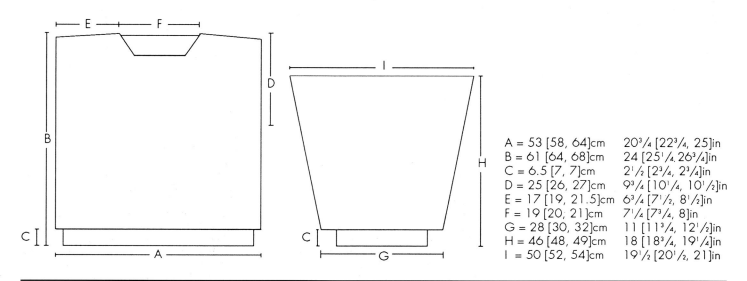

A = 53 [58, 64]cm   20¾ [22¾, 25]in
B = 61 [64, 68]cm   24 [25¼, 26¾]in
C = 6.5 [7, 7]cm   2½ [2¾, 2¾]in
D = 25 [26, 27]cm   9¾ [10¼, 10½]in
E = 17 [19, 21.5]cm   6¾ [7½, 8½]in
F = 19 [20, 21]cm   7¼ [7¾, 8]in
G = 28 [30, 32]cm   11 [11¾, 12½]in
H = 46 [48, 49]cm   18 [18¾, 19¼]in
I = 50 [52, 54]cm   19½ [20½, 21]in

Multi-coloured ribbing, worked in a striped and check pattern, makes a perfect finishing touch at the edges of this beautiful sweater.

FRONT

As back to within 18[20,22] rows of beg of shoulder shaping, with right side facing for next row.

Shape Neck and Shoulders

Working next row of chart, patt 66[72,80] sts; place the next 19 [21,21] sts on a holder; leave the rem sts on a spare needle.

Turn, and keeping continuity of patt, work the first set of sts, shaping left neck as follows:-

** Cast off 3 sts at beg of next and foll alt row. Cast off 2 sts at beg of next 4 alt rows. Dec 1 st at beg of next 3[4,5] alt rows. 49[54,61] sts **.

With right side facing, shape shoulder by casting off 16[18,20] sts at beg of next and foll alt row . Patt 1 row straight, then cast off the rem 17[18,21] sts.

With right side facing, rejoin A to the 66[72,80] sts of right side and, keeping continuity, patt 2 rows straight. Work as left neck from ** to **. With wrong side facing, begin shoulder shaping on next row and complete to match left shoulder.

SLEEVES

With 2¾mm (US2) needles and A, cast on 64[68,72] sts. Work 2/2 rib as back and front until cuff measures 6.5[7,7]cm 2½[2¾, 2¾]in, with wrong side facing for next row.

Next Row – Increase

First and 2nd Sizes: K4[2], * m1, k4; rep from * to the last 4 [2] sts; m1, k4[2]. 79[85] sts.

3rd Size: K1, * m1, k4; rep from * tô the last 3 sts; m1, k2, m1, k1. 91 sts.

All Sizes: Change to 3¼mm (US3) needles and, joining in and breaking off colours as required, work patt from chart, repeating the 30 patt sts 2[2,3] times, and working the first 9[12,0] sts and the last 10[13,1] sts on right side rows, and the first 10[13,1] sts and the last 9[12,0] on wrong side rows as indicated on chart.

Continue as set, and inc 1 st at each end of every 4th row, working increased sts into patt, until there are 141 [147,153] sts. Continue straight in patt until sleeve

measures 46[48,49]cm 18[18¾,19¼]in. With A, cast off all sts.

FINISHING

Do not press garment pieces. With A, join back and front at shoulder seams. Press seams lightly on wrong side.

Neckband

With 2¾mm (US2) double-pointed or circular needles and A, pick up and k the 47[51,53] sts from back neck holder; knit up 33[34,35] sts evenly to front holder; pick up and k the 19[21,21] sts from front holder; knit up 33[34,35] sts evenly to

complete rnd. 132[140,144] sts. Work 8 rnds in 2/2 rib as follows:-

Rnds 1 & 2: K2 A, p2 C.

Rnds 3 & 4: K2 A, p2 E.

Rnds 5 & 6: K2 A, p2 G.

Rnds 7 & 8: K2 A, p2 H.

With A, cast off loosely, knitwise. Place markers on back and front 25[26,27]cm 9¾ [10¼,10½]in from shoulder seam. Place centre top of sleeves at shoulder seams and, with A, sew sleeves to body between markers. Press seams lightly on wrong side. With A, sew up side and sleeve seams. Press seams lightly on wrong side, omitting ribs.

ARDAGH
CHILD'S SWEATER
IN CELTIC FRETWORK

RATING

★ ★

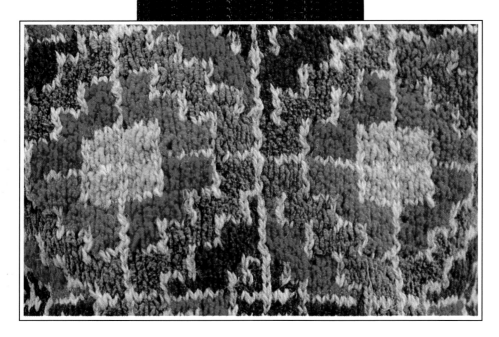

The large squared grid of Ardagh, with its diamond overlay, lends itself well to all kinds of colour schemes. For the child's version of this sweater I have used a variety of brighter shades from the more playful images in the Book of Kells.

SIZES
To fit age 6-7[8-9] yrs or chest 61-64[66-69]cm 24-25 [26-27]in.
Directions for larger size are given in parenthesis. Where there is only one set of figures, it applies to both sizes.

KNITTED MEASUREMENTS
Underarm 73[83]cm 28½[32½]in.
Length from top of shoulder 42[45]cm 16½[17¾]in.
Sleeve length 33[35.5]cm 13[14]in.

MATERIALS
Yarn: Rowan Donegal Tweed; Rowan Fine Cotton Chenille.

A. Oatmeal Donegal Tweed (469) 50[75]g;
B. Turquoise Fine Chenille (383) 50g;
C. Seville Fine Chenille (387) 50g; **D.** Gorse Fine Chenille (391) 25g; **E.** Cardinal Fine Chenille (379) 25[50]g; **F.** Willow Fine Chenille (395) 50g; **G.** Cyclamen Fine Chenille (385) 50g; **H.** Flamenco Fine Chenille (398) 25[50]g; **I.** Privet Fine Chenille (394) 25g.

1 Pair each 2¾mm (US2) and 3¼mm (US3) needles. 1 Set of double-pointed or 40cm (16in) circular 2¾ (US2) needles. 2 Stitch holders. Stitch markers. Darning needle.

TENSION (GAUGE)
29 sts and 33 rows to 10cm (4in), measured over chart patt, using 3¼mm (US3) needles.

STITCHES
2/2 rib: K2 with first colour, p2 with second colour, stranding the yarns evenly across the wrong side. **Chart patt**: Worked entirely in st.st. beg with a k row. Odd numbered rows are right side, even are wrong side. Yarn A is carried across all rows. Use separate lengths of yarn for each contrast area. Approx. 92cm (36in) lengths of B and F; 81cm (32in) of C and E; 64cm (25in) of G and H; 46cm (18in) of D; 38cm (15in) of I, will be sufficient to knit each separate area of contrast colour, with enough to weave in or darn in at beg and end. Before working each contrast area, wrap the contrast yarn around A on every row, to avoid gaps. See page 137 for intarsia knitting.

BACK
With 2¾mm (US2) needles and A, cast on 92[104] sts. Joining in and breaking off colours as required, work 2/2 rib as follows :-
Row 1: K2 A, p2 B. **Row 2**: K2 B, p2 A.
Row 3: K2 A, p2 C. **Row 4**: K2 C, p2 A.
Row 5: K2 A, p2 F. **Row 6**: K2 F, p2 A.
Row 7: K2 A, p2 G. **Row 8**: K2 G, p2 A.
Repeat this sequence until rib measures 4.5[5]cm 1¾[2] in, with wrong side facing for next row.

Next row – Increase: With A, p4, * m1, p7[6]; rep from * to the last 4 sts; m1, p4. 105[121] sts.

Change to 3¼mm (US3) needles, and joining in and breaking off colours as required, work the patt from chart, repeating the 30 patt sts 3[4] times, and working the first 7[0] sts and the last 8[1] sts on right side rows, and the first 8[1] sts and the last 7[0] sts on wrong side rows, as indicated on chart.

For a child, lighter coloured outlines to the shapes define the brighter colours they enclose, yet the complete effect is softer and more appealing.

Girls and boys will both love this jolly sweater with its paintbox colouring.

Continue straight as set, repeating the 30 patt rows until back measures 41[44]cm 16¼[17½]in from beg, with right side facing for next row.

Shape Neck and Shoulders
Working next row of chart, patt 33[39] sts; place the next 39[43] sts on a holder. Turn, and keeping continuity of patt, work the first set of sts, and dec 1 st at beg of next and foll 2 alt rows. AT THE SAME TIME, when back measures 42[45]cm 16½[17¾]in with right side facing for next row, shape shoulders by casting off with A, 10[12] sts at beg of next 3 alt rows.

With right side facing, rejoin yarn, and keeping continuity, patt the rem 33[39] sts of left shoulder. Dec 1 st at neck edge of

CHART A

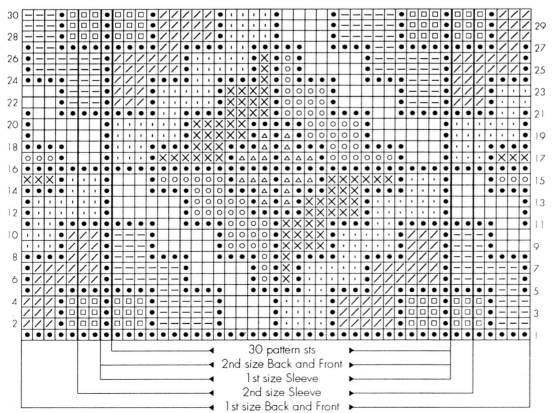

KEY

⦁ = A
□ = B
⊟ = C
▣ = D
◨ = E
⎸ = F
☒ = G
○ = H
△ = I

30 pattern sts
2nd size Back and Front
1st size Sleeve
2nd size Sleeve
1st size Back and Front

next 3 alt rows and with wrong side facing, shape shoulder to match right.

FRONT
As back to within 15[17] rows of beg of shoulder shaping, with right side facing for next row.

Shape Neck and Shoulders
Working next row of chart, patt 45[52] sts; place the next 15[17] sts on a holder; leave rem sts on a spare needle.
Turn, and keeping continuity of patt, work the first set of sts, shaping left neck as follows :-
** Cast off 3 sts at beg of next and foll alt row. Cast off 2 sts at beg of next 3 alt rows. Dec 1 st at beg of next 3[4] alt rows **.

Next row: With right side facing, cast off 10[12] sts with A, and keeping continuity, patt to end of row. Patt 1 row straight. Rep these last 2 rows. With A, cast off the rem 10[12] sts.

With right side facing, rejoin yarn to the 45[52] sts on spare needle, and keeping continuity, patt 2 rows. Work as left neck from ** to **. With wrong side facing,

begin shoulder shaping on next row, and complete to match left shoulder.

SLEEVES
With 2¾mm (US2) needles and A, cast on 52[56] sts. Work 2/2 rib as on back and front until cuff measures 4.5[5]cm 1¾[2]in, with wrong side facing for next row.
Next row – Increase: First size: P2 * m1, p6; rep from * to the last 2 sts; m1, p2. 61 sts.
Second size: P1, * m1, p7; rep from * to the last 6 sts; m1, p5, m1, p1. 65 sts.
Both sizes: Change to 3¼mm (US3) needles, and joining in and breaking off colours as required, work the patt from chart, repeating the 30 patt sts twice, and working the first 0[2] sts and the last 1[3] sts on right side rows, and the first 1[3] sts and the last 0[2] sts on wrong side rows, as indicated on chart.

Continue as set, and inc 1 st at each end of every 3rd row until there are 87[101] sts, then inc 1 st at each end of every foll 4th row until there are 107[117] sts, working all increased sts into patt. Continue straight in patt until sleeve measures

33[35.5]cm 13[14]in from beg. Cast off all sts with A.

FINISHING
Do not press garment pieces. With A, backstitch back and front together at shoulders. Press seams lightly on wrong side.

Neckband
With 2¾mm (US2) double-pointed or circular needles and A, pick up and k 39[43] sts from back holder; knit up 31[32] sts to front holder; pick up and k 15[17] sts from holder; knit up 31[32] sts to complete round. 116[124] sts. Work 6 rnds in 2/2 rib as follows:-
Rnds 1 & 2: K2 A, p2 F. **Rnds 3 & 4**: K2 A, p2 C. **Rnds 5 & 6**: K2 A, p2 B. With A, cast off loosely, knitwise.

Place markers on back and front 18.5[20.5]cm 7¼[8]in from shoulder seam. Place centre top of sleeves at shoulder seams, and with A, backstitch sleeves to body between markers. Press seams lightly on wrong side. With A, backstitch side and sleeve seams. Press seams lightly on wrong side, omitting ribs.

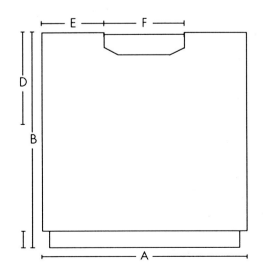

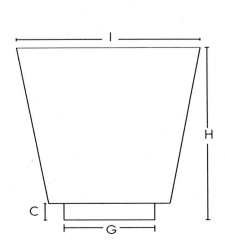

A = 36.5 [41.5]cm   14¼ [16¾]in
B = 42 [45]cm   16½ [17¾]in
C = 4.5 [5]cm   1¾ [2]in
D = 18.5 [20]cm   7¼ [8]in
E = 10.25 [12.25]cm   4 [4¾]in
F = 16 [17]cm   6¼ [6¾]in
G = 21.5 [23]cm   8½ [9]in
H = 33 [35.5]cm   13 [14]in
I = 37 [41]cm   14½ [16]in

KELLS
SWEATER IN CELTIC FRETWORK

RATING

SIZES

To fit chest/bust 81-91[97-107,112-117]cm 32-36[38-42,44-46]in.
Directions for larger sizes are given in parenthesis. Where there is only one set of figures, it applies to all sizes.

KNITTED MEASUREMENTS

Underarm 104[116,132]cm 41[46,52]in.
Length from top of shoulder 63.5[66.5,69]cm 25[26¼, 27¼]in.
Sleeve length 47[49,51]cm 18½[19¼,20]in.

MATERIALS

Yarn: Rowan DDK; Lambswool Tweed; Kid/Silk; Rowan LDK.

A. Holly Kid/Silk (990) 50g; **B.** Dark Emerald DDK (658) 100g; **C.** Kohl Lambswool Tweed (185) 200g; **D.** Navy DDK (628) 100g; **E.** Steel Blue Kid/Silk (991) 25g; **F.** Old Gold Kid/Silk (989) 75g; **G.** Olive DDK (407) 50g; **H.** Smoke Kid/Silk (998) 25g; **I.** Garnet Kid/Silk (992) 50g; **J.** Potpourri Kid/Silk (996) 25g; **K.** Crushed Berry Kid/Silk (993) 75g; **L.** Deep Violet DDK (652) 50g; **N.** Rose Pink DDK (70) 50g; **O.** Ruby Red DDK (651) 50g; **P.** Pillar Box LDK (45) 50g; **Q.** Rust DDK (662) 50g; **R.** Red Rust DDK (627) 100g; **S.** Russet DDK (663) 100g.

1 Pair each 3¾mm (US5) and 4mm (US6) needles. 1 Set of double-pointed or 40cm 16in circular 3¾mm (US5) needle. 2 Stitch holders. Stitch markers. Darning needle.

TENSION (GAUGE)

25 sts and 27 rows to 10cm (4in), measured over chart patt, using 4mm (US6) needles.

Combining 18 colours and a luxurious mixture of kid/silk and woollen yarns produces this spectacular designer sweater.

STITCHES

2/2 rib: K2 with first colour, p2 with second colour, stranding the yarns evenly across the wrong side. **Chart patt**: Worked entirely in st.st. beg with a k row. Odd numbered rows are right side, even numbered rows are wrong side. Yarns A,B,C,D, and E are carried across rows on which they are worked. Use separate lengths of yarn for each contrast colour area. Before working each contrast area, wrap the contrast yarn around the carried yarn on every row, to avoid gaps. See page 137 for intarsia knitting.

BACK

With 3¾mm (US5) needles and C, cast on 112[128,144] sts. Joining in and breaking off colours as required, work 2/2 rib as follows :-
Row 1: K2 C, p2 O. **Row 2**: K2 O, p2 C.
Row 3: K2 C, p2 R. **Row 4**: K2 R, p2 C.
Row 5: K2 C, p2 I. **Row 6**: K2 I, p2 C.
Row 7: K2 C, p2 K. **Row 8**: K2 K, p2 C.
Row 9: K2 C, p2 F. **Row 10**: K2 F, p2 C.
Rep from row 1 until rib measures 6[7,7]cm 2½[2¾, 2¾]in, with wrong side facing for next row.

Next row – Increase: With C, p1, m1, p7, * m1, p8; rep from * to the last 8 sts; m1, p7, m1, p1. 127[145,163] sts.

Change to 4mm (US6) needles, and joining in and breaking off colours as required, work 148[154,162] rows from chart B (foll chart A for detail).

Shape Shoulders and Neck
Continue to work from chart and cast off 13[16,19]sts; patt the next 29[34,39]sts; place the next 43[45,47] sts on a holder. Turn and work the first 29[34,39] sts as follows:-
Dec 1 st at beg of next row. Cast off 13[16,19] sts at beg of next row. **First size only**: Dec 1 st at beg of next row. **Second and Third sizes**: Patt 1 row straight. **All sizes**: Cast off the rem 14[17,19] sts.

With right side facing, work from chart and patt across the rem 29[34,39] sts. Continue working from chart and patt the next row straight, and shape shoulder and neck to match previous side.

The Book of Kells is without doubt the most splendid of all the Celtic manuscripts. Its pages explode with an almost unbelievable maze of incredibly fine and gorgeously coloured patterns that I find irresistible. For the practical purpose of knitting, I chose a small repetitive motif which fills a diamond shape of about three centimetres on one of the pages. For this sweater I repeated the shape, then threw in rich colours of yarn, virtually at random, to give an impression of exotic profusion. You can work the colours exactly as I have done, though you may find it more relaxing to use them at will.

CHART B

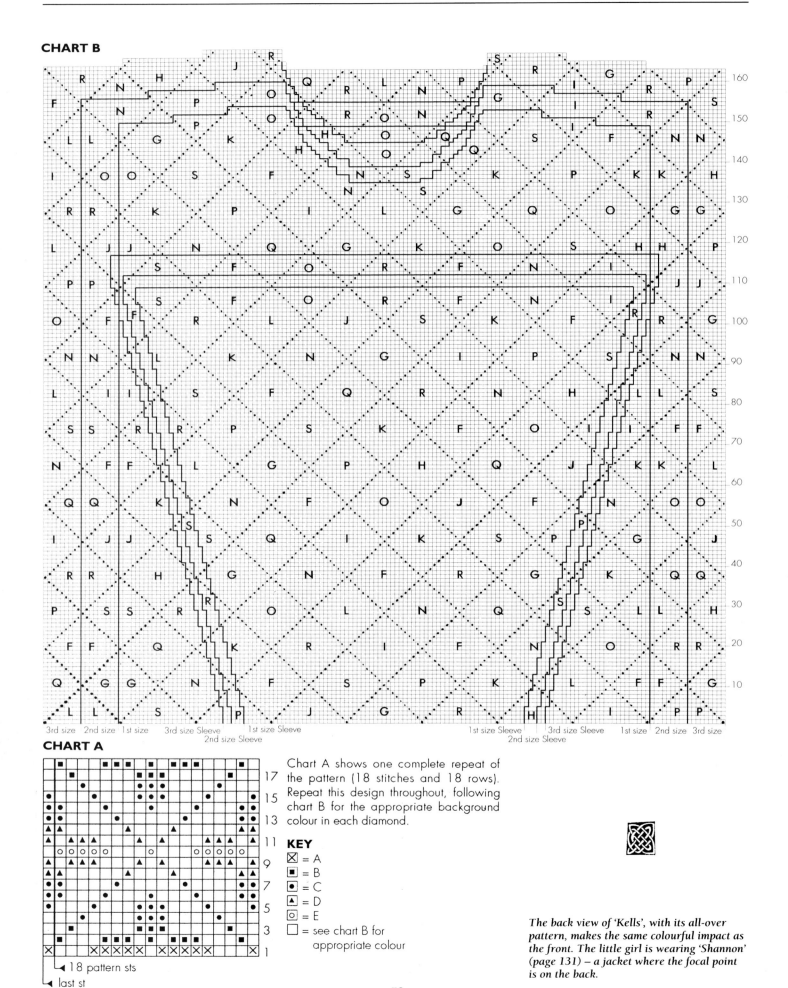

3rd size 2nd size 1st size 3rd size Sleeve 1st size Sleeve 1st size Sleeve 3rd size Sleeve 1st size 2nd size 3rd size
2nd size Sleeve 2nd size Sleeve

CHART A

17
15
13
11
9
7
5
3
1

◄ 18 pattern sts

◄ last st

Chart A shows one complete repeat of the pattern (18 stitches and 18 rows). Repeat this design throughout, following chart B for the appropriate background colour in each diamond.

KEY

⊠ = A
▪ = B
• = C
▲ = D
⊙ = E
☐ = see chart B for appropriate colour

The back view of 'Kells', with its all-over pattern, makes the same colourful impact as the front. The little girl is wearing 'Shannon' (page 131) – a jacket where the focal point is on the back.

52

FRONT

As back, but working 134[138,144] rows of chart.

Shape Neck and Shoulders
Continue working from chart and patt 55[64,72] sts; place the next 17[17,19] sts on a holder; leave the rem sts on a spare needle . Turn and work the first 55[64,72] sts as follows:-
** Continue working from chart, cast off 3 sts at beg of next row and 2 sts at beg of next 2 alt rows. Dec 1 st at neck edge of next 4 rows. Dec 1 st at neck edge of next 4 alt rows, and shape shoulder as back when indicated on chart. **

With right side facing, work from chart and patt across the rem 55[64,72] sts. Continue working from chart and patt 1 row straight, then shape neck and shoulders as previous side, from ** to **.

SLEEVES

With 3¾mm (US5) needles and C, cast on 56[60,64] sts. Work 2/2 rib as back and front until rib measures 6[7,7]cm 2½[2¾, 2¾]in, with wrong side facing for next row.

Next row – Increase: P3[6,2], *m1, p5[4,5]; rep from * to the last 3[6,2] sts; m1, p3[6,2]. 67[73,77] sts.

Change to 4mm (US6) needles and work patt from chart, as indicated, increasing 1 st at each end of 5th and every foll 4th row until there are 119[125,131] sts. Work 3[6,7] rows straight in patt. Cast off all sts.

FINISHING

Press all pieces lightly on wrong side, omitting ribs. With B, backstitch back and front together at shoulders. Press seams lightly on wrong side.

NECKBAND

With right side facing, 3¾mm (US5) needles and C, pick up and k the 43[45,47] sts from back neck holder; knit up 22[25,27] sts evenly to front neck holder; pick up the 17[17,19] sts from holder; knit up 22[25,27] sts evenly to complete round. 104[112,120] sts. Work 2/2 rib as follows:-
Rnds 1 and 2: K2 C, p2 K. **Rnds 3 and 4**: K2 C, p2 I. **Rnds 5 and 6**: K2 C, p2 R.

Rnds 7 and 8: K2 C, p2 O. With C, cast off loosely and evenly, knitwise.

Place markers at back and front 24[25.5,26.5]cm 9½[10, 10½]in from shoulder seam. Place centre top of sleeves at shoulder seams, and with B, backstitch sleeves to body between markers. Press seams lightly on wrong side. With B, backstitch side and sleeve seams. Press seams lightly on wrong side, omitting ribs.

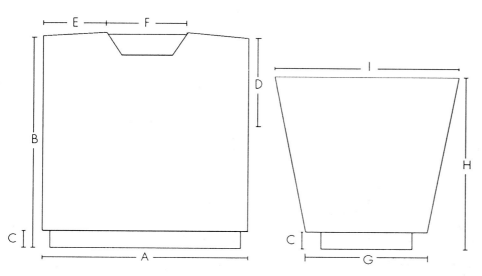

A = 52 [58, 66]cm	20½ [23, 26]in
B = 63.5 [66.5, 69]cm	25 [26¼, 27¼]in
C = 6 [7, 7]cm	2½ [2¾, 2¾]in
D = 24 [25.5, 26.5]cm	9½ [10, 10½]in
E = 16.5 [20, 23]cm	6½ [7¾, 9]in
F = 19 [19, 20]cm	7½ [7½, 8]in
G = 27 [29, 31.5]cm	10¾ [11½, 12½]in
H = 47 [49, 51]cm	18½ [19¼, 20]in
I = 48 [51, 53]cm	19[20, 21]in

DALMORE
SLIPOVER
IN CELTIC FRETWORK

RATING

★ ★

SIZES
To fit bust/chest 86-92[102-107]cm
34-36[40-42]in.
Directions for larger size are given in parenthesis. Where there is only one set of figures, it applies to both sizes.

KNITTED MEASUREMENTS
Underarm 102[114]cm 40[45]in.
Length from top of shoulder 57[63]
22½[24¾]in.

MATERIALS
Yarn: Rowan Donegal Lambswool Tweed;
Silk/Wool; Silkstones; Wool/Cotton.

A. Pickle Donegal Tweed (483) 50[70]g;
B. Bramble Donegal Tweed (484) 50g;
C. Elderberry Donegal Tweed (490) 50g;
D. Sapphire Donegal Tweed (486) 25g;
E. Roseberry Donegal Tweed (480) 25g;
F. Pine Silk/Wool (860) 40g; **G.** Moss Green Silk/Wool (852) 40g; **H.** Donkey Silk/Wool (856) 40[60]g; **I.** Silkstones Dried Rose (825) 50g; **J.** Mulberry Silkstones (836) 50g; **K.** Musk Wool/Cotton (913) 80g.

1 Set of double pointed or circular 2¾mm (US2) and 3¼mm (US3) needles. 3 Stitch holders. Stitch markers. 1 Safety pin. 1 Darner.

TENSION (GAUGE)
16 sts and 18 rows to 5cm (2in), measured over chart patt using 3¼mm (US3) needles, and working on right side only, breaking off yarns at the end of every row. See page 137 for working a Fair Isle swatch.

STITCHES
2/2 rib: K2 with the first colour, p2 with the second colour, stranding the yarns evenly across wrong side. **Chart patt**: K every round and on two-colour rounds, strand the yarn not in immediate use evenly across wrong side. On stretches of more than 7 sts in one colour, weave in yarn not in use at centre of stretch. **Steeks**: Worked at armholes and front and back neck, and later cut up centre to form openings. The steek is worked over 10 sts. K these sts on every round, and on two-colour rounds, k each st and round in alt colours. Do not weave in newly joined or broken off yarns at centre of first steek.

The pattern on this slipover is taken from a single border on an illuminated manuscript from Lindisfarne, a tiny island off the coast of Northumberland, North East England. The regular character of the border makes it an excellent Fair Isle design - one that can be repeated across the width of the knitting and for the length of the fabric. Worked here in a subtle mix of tweed and silk and wool yarns, this garment will be popular with both men and women.

Instead leave approx. 5cm 2in tail when joining in and breaking off yarns. **Cross stitch**: With darner, overcast raw edge of steek to strands on wrong side, and after sewing to end, reverse to form cross stitches. See page 137 for full illustrations of steeks and cross stitch.

BODY
With 2¾mm (US2) needles and yarn A, cast on 300[336] sts. Mark the first st of rnd, and making sure cast on edge is not twisted, work 2/2 rib as follows:-
Rnds 1 and 2: K2 A, p2 G. **Rnd 3**: K2 A, p2 H. **Rnd 4**: K2 B, p2 H. **Rnd 5**: K2 B, p2 I. **Rnds 6 and 7**: K2 C, p2 I. **Rnd 8**: K2 C, p2 K. **Rnds 9 and 10**: K2 D, p2 K. **Rnd 11** K2 D, p2 J. **Rnds 12 and 13**: K2 F, p2 J. **Rnd 14**: K2 F, p2 E. **Rnds 15 through 17**: As rnd 13 working back through rnd 1.

Next Rnd – Increase
With yarn A, * k15[14], m1; rep from * to end of rnd. 320[360] sts. Mark the first and centre sts of rnd. 159[179] sts between marked sts.

Change to 3¼mm (US3) needles and, joining in and breaking off colours as required, work the patt from chart, repeating the 20 patt sts 16[18] times in the rnd.
Repeat the 20 patt rnds and work 99[115] rnds in total. Break off yarns.

CHART A

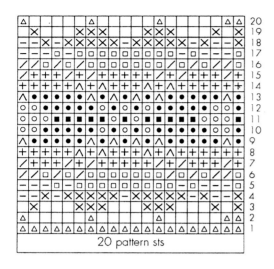

20 pattern sts

A = 102 [114]cm
B = 57 [63]cm
C = 6cm
D = 34 [39]cm
E = 23 [24]cm
F = 9.5 [10]cm
G = 18.5 [19.5]cm

A = 40 [45]in
B = 22½ [24¾]in
C = 2½in
D = 13½ [15¼]in
E = 9 [9½]in
F = 3¾ [4]in
G = 7¼ [7¾]in

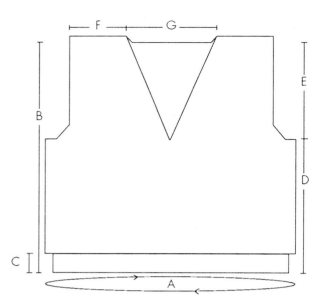

KEY

□ = A	◪ = D	◪ = G	⊡ = J
⊟ = B	◪ = E	◪ = H	⊞ = K
◪ = C	◉ = F	◪ = I	

Shape Armholes and Work Steeks
Place the last 9[11] sts and the first 10[12] sts of rnd on a holder; first st of rnd will be centre st on holder; with alt colours as for next rnd of chart patt, cast on 5 steek sts, marking the first st cast on for beg of rnd; keeping continuity, patt 141 [157] sts; place the next 19[23] sts on a holder; centre st of rnd will be the centre st on holder; with alt colours, cast on 10 steek sts; keeping continuity, patt the rem 141[157] sts; with alt colours, cast on 5 steek sts.

Work steeks with alt colours, and keeping continuity of chart patt, dec 1 st at each side of both steeks on next 9 rnds. 123[139] patt sts rem between steeks.
Next Rnd – Begin Neck Shaping
Keeping continuity, k5 steek sts; patt 61[69]; place the next st (centre front st) on a safety pin; with alt colours, cast on 10 steek sts; keeping continuity, work as set to end of rnd.
Keeping continuity, dec 1 st at each side of armhole and front neck steeks on next and foll alt rnds 4[6] times in all. 115[127] patt sts rem on back. Then work straight at armholes and continue to dec 1 st at each side of front neck steek on alt rnds until 41[45] patt sts rem at each side of front neck steek. Then continue to dec at neck on every foll 3rd rnd until 29[33] patt sts rem at each side of front neck steek. AT THE SAME TIME, on rnd 12 of 9th[10th] rnd rep of chart from beg, shape back neck as follows:-
Continue as set to back patt sts; patt 32[36]; place the next 51[55] sts on a

holder; with alt colours, cast on 10 steek sts; keeping continuity, work to end of rnd. Continue as set for front neck steek and dec 1 st at each side of back neck steek on next and foll alt rnds 3 times in all. 29[33] sts rem between steeks. Continue straight in patt, ending after rnd 19 of chart. Work rnd 20 of chart, casting off all steek sts on this rnd. With yarn G, graft shoulder sts together. See page 137 for grafting. With yarn A, sew backstitch up centre of first and last sts of all steeks.

FINISHING
Cut open front and back neck steeks up centre, between 5th and 6th steek sts.

NECKBAND
With 2¾mm (US2) needles, yarn C, and working into patt st next to steek, knit up 78[82] sts evenly up right front neck edge to back neck holder; pick up and k the 51[55] sts from holder and dec 1 st at centre back neck; knit up 78[82] sts evenly down left front neck edge; pick up and k the st from safety pin. 207[219] sts.
Working 2/2 rib in colours as rnd 6 back through rnd 1 of body, shape neckband as follows:-
Rnd 1: * K2, p2; rep from * to the last 3 sts of rnd; k1; sl 2 sts TOGETHER – k1 (first st of next rnd) - pass the 2 slipped sts over the k st. **Rnd 2**: K1, * p2, k2; rep from * to the last 4 sts; p2; sl2 TOGETHER-k1-p2sso. **Rnd 3**: * P2, k2; rep from * to the last 3 sts; p1; sl2 TOGETHER-k1-p2sso. **Rnd 4**: P1, * k2, p2; rep from * to the last 4 sts; k2; sl2 TOGETHER-k1-p2sso. Work rnds 1 and

2 once more. With yarn A, cast off loosely and evenly, knitwise.

ARMHOLE BANDS
Cut open armhole steeks up centre between 5th and 6th steek sts. With 2¾mm (US2) needles and yarn C, beg at centre st on holder and pick up and k the last 10[12] sts from holder; working into patt st next to steek, knit up 145[153] sts evenly around armhole; pick up and k the rem 9[11] sts from holder. 164[176] sts. Mark the first st of rnd and, with colours as for neckband, work 6 rnds of 2/2 rib. With yarn A, cast off evenly, knitwise. Trim all steeks to a 3 st width and cross st in position. Darn in all loose ends. Press lightly on wrong side, omitting ribs.

The muted shades of yarn used for this slipover blend perfectly with the Irish landscape. Bands of patterns featuring symmetrical motifs in ever-changing colours are typical of Fair Isle design.

CELTIC
KNOTWORK

CROMARTY
SWEATER
IN CELTIC KNOTWORK

RATING

★ ★

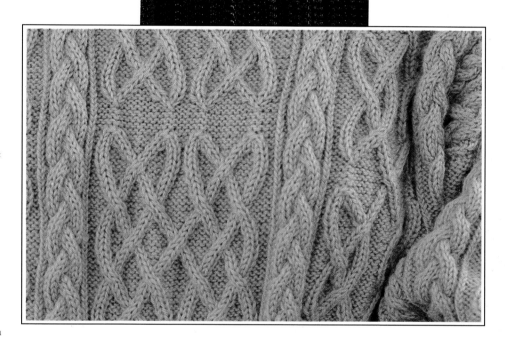

SIZES
One size fits bust 86-97cm 34-38in.

KNITTED MEASUREMENTS
Underarm 114cm 45in.
Length from top of shoulder 57cm 22in.
Sleeve length 43cm 17in.

MATERIALS
Yarn: 15 50g balls of Rowan DDK in shade no. 665 (Ice Blue). 1 Pair 3¾mm (US5) needles. 1 Cable needle. Stitch marker. Darner.

TENSION (GAUGE)
25 sts and 31 rows to 10cm (4in), measured over st.st., using 3¾mm (US5) needles.

STITCHES
Chart patts: Odd numbered rows are right side, and even numbered rows are wrong side. The cabled sts are worked in st.st. on a reverse st.st. background, as indicated on charts. **Note**: The stitch number in charts C and D increases at the beginning and decreases to the original number at the end of each panel. This is indicated on the charts.

BACK AND FRONT
(2 alike)
With 3¾mm (US5) needles, cast on 184 sts. Working from row 1 of all charts, set the patts as follows:-
Row 1: K1; k1b; chart A over the next 13 sts; k1b; chart B over the next 8 sts; k1b; chart A over the next 13 sts; k1b; chart C over the next 23 sts, increasing as indicated; k1b; chart A over the next 13

The wonderful variety of textures depicted in this harsh country scene is reflected in the richly textured surface of 'Cromarty'. Cables and travelling stitches are embossed against a reverse stocking stitch fabric.

The Celtic crosses suggested the strong vertical panels and square shaping of this sweater, while the icy blue colour and textured surface reflect the stone material. I used a unit of knotwork from the Nigg stone for the sweater's centre panel. The side and centre sleeve panels have a typical pattern found on numerous Pictish stones in Eastern Scotland.

sts; k1b; chart D over the next 30 sts; k1b; chart A over the next 13 sts; k1b; chart C over the next 23 sts, increasing as indicated; k1b; chart A over the next 13 sts; k1b; chart E over the next 8 sts; k1b; chart A over the next 13 sts; k1b; k1.
Row 2: K1; p1b; chart A; p1b; chart E; p1b; chart A; p1b; chart C; p1b; chart A; p1b; chart D; p1b; chart A; p1b; chart C; p1b; chart A; p1b; chart B; p1b; chart A; p1b; k1.

Continue as set and repeat the 4 rows of charts B and E and the 8 rows of chart A. After working the 30 rows of chart C once, repeat from row 3. Repeat the 40 rows of chart D 4 times from beg, then continue as set for 2 more rows, working rows 1 and 2 of chart D.

Shape Neck
Keeping continuity, patt charts A, B, A, and C; k1; cast off the next 56 sts, decreasing 1 st at centre of both chart A patts during cast off; k1; keeping continuity, patt the rem sts. Turn, and keeping continuity, patt each shoulder separately, working k1 at the neck edge of every row. Continue straight through row 28 of chart C. Then patt row 29 of chart C but s1 dec the 5 centre sts together on this row. Work 1 more row as set and k all 23 sts of chart C. Cast off all sts, decreasing 3 sts evenly spaced over both chart A patts, and 1 st at centre of chart E patt.

CHART A

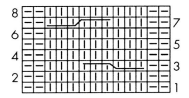

CHART C

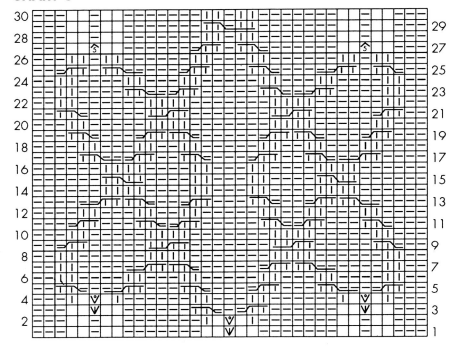

CHART B

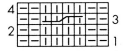

KEY

☐ = no stitch

Ⅰ = k on RS rows and p on WS rows

⊟ = p on RS rows and k on WS rows

Ⅴ = (k1b, k1) in one st, then insert left hand needle point behind the vertical strand that runs down between the 2 sts just made and k into this strand making the 3rd st of the group

Ⅴ = (p1, yo, p1) into one st, making 3 sts in the group

⑤ = slip decrease 5 sts together thus: sl 3 knitwise, one at a time, with yarn at back, drop yarn then *pass the 2nd st on right hand needle over the first (centre) st: sl the centre st back to left hand needle and pass the next st on left

hand needle over it*; sl the centre st back to right hand needle and rep from * to * once more: p the centre st to complete the decrease

⊟⤢ⅠⅠ = put the first st on cn and hold at back: k the next 2 sts, then p the st from cn

ⅠⅠ⤢⊟ = put the first 2 sts on cn and hold at front: p the next st, then k the 2 sts from cn

⊟⤢ⅠⅠ = put the first 2 sts on cn and hold at back, k the next 2 sts, then p the 2 sts from cn

ⅠⅠ⤢⊟ = put the first 2 sts on cn and hold at front: p the next 2 sts, then k the 2 sts from cn

ⅠⅠ⤢ⅠⅠ = put the first 2 sts on cn and hold at back: k the next 2 sts, then k the 2 sts from cn

ⅠⅠ⤢ⅠⅠ = put the first 2 sts on cn and hold at front: k the next 2 sts, then k the 2 sts from cn

ⅠⅠⅠ⤢ⅠⅠ = put the first 3 sts on cn and hold at front: k the next 2 sts, sl the p st back onto left hand needle and p it, then k the 2 sts from cn

ⅠⅠⅠ⤢ⅠⅠⅠ = put the first 3 sts on cn and hold at back: k the next 3 sts, then k the 3 sts from cn

ⅠⅠⅠ⤢ⅠⅠⅠ = put the first 3 sts on cn and hold at front: k the next 3 sts, then k the 3 sts from cn

A = 57cm   22½in
B = 50cm   19¾in
C = 21.5cm   8½in
D = 19.5cm   7¾in
E = 18cm   7in
F = 23cm   9in
G = 21.5cm   8½in
H = 11.5cm   4½in
I = 43cm   17in

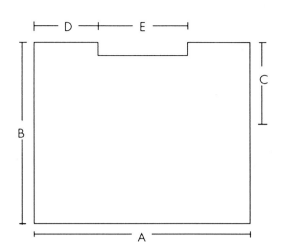

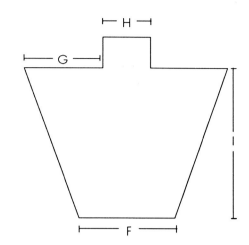

CHART E

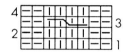

CHART D

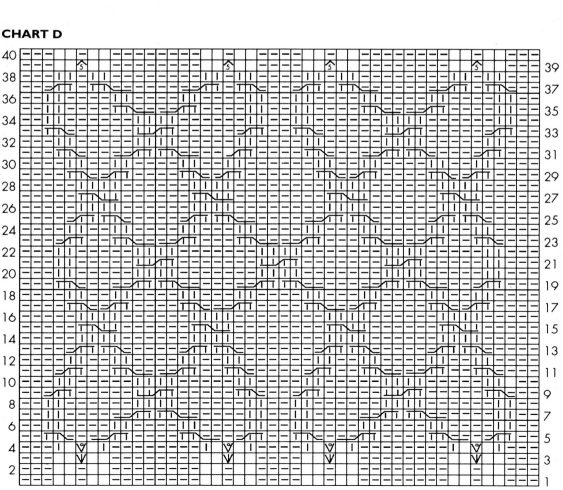

Place stitch markers at each side, 21.5cm 8½in from shoulder cast off.

SLEEVES

With 3¾mm (US5) needles, cast on 75 sts. Working all charts from row 1, set the patt as follows:-
Row 1: P2; k1b; chart B over the next 8 sts; k1b; chart A over the next 13 sts; k1b; chart C over the next 23 sts, increasing as indicated; k1b; chart A over the next 13 sts; k1b; chart E over the next 8 sts; k1b; p2.
Row 2: K2; p1b; chart E; p1b; chart A; p1b; chart C; p1b; chart A; p1b; chart B; p1b; k2.

Continue as set and rep the 4 rows of charts B and E, and the 8 rows of chart A. After working the 30 rows of chart C, repeat from row 3. Shape the sleeve by increasing 1 st at each side of every 4th row, working all increased sts in reverse st.st. until there are 37 reverse st.st. at each side of first and last k1b. Then continue straight as set until 144 patt rows have been worked from beg, working through row 4 of 6th chart C rep.

Shape Saddle
Cast off 58 sts, decreasing 1 st at centre of chart B patt, and 3 sts evenly spaced over chart A sts; k1; keeping continuity, patt to end of row. **Next row:** Cast off 58 sts, decreasing 1 st at centre of chart B sts and 3 sts evenly spaced over chart A sts; k1; keeping continuity, patt the rem sts. Continue straight in patt over the rem sts, working k1 at each end of every row. Work straight through row 28 of 8th chart C rep, from beg. On row 29 slip dec the 5 centre sts together. Work 8 more rows as set, working reverse st.st. over the 23 centre sts. Cast off evenly.

FINISHING

Do not press pieces. Sew sides of sleeve saddles to back and front shoulders. Sew top of sleeves to body, between markers. Sew up side and sleeve seams.

NECKBAND

With 3¾mm (US5) needles, cast on 12 sts.

Row 1: (right side) k1; k1b; work chart B over the next 8 sts; k1b; k1. **Row 2:** K1; p1b; chart B; p1b; k1.

Continue as set and rep the 4 rows of chart B. Make 2 bands to fit across neck cast off. Sew in position. Then make 2 bands to fit along shoulder edges, between the first 2 bands. Sew in position, joining ends to the first 2 bands.

Here the centre sleeve panel, with a typical knotwork pattern, extends into the shoulder saddle. The square neckline is bordered with strips of cable edging.

66

DURROW
SWEATER
IN CELTIC KNOTWORK

RATING

SIZES
To fit chest/bust 91-97[101-107,112-117]cm
36-38 [40-42,44-46]in.
Directions for larger sizes are given in
parenthesis. Where there is only one set of
figures, it applies to all sizes.

KNITTED MEASUREMENTS
Underarm 109[117,125]cm 43[46,49]in.
Length from top of shoulder 64[66,68]cm
25¼[26,26¾]in.
Sleeve length 47[48,49]cm 18½[19,19¼]in.

MATERIALS
Yarn: Rowan Donegal Tweed; Rowan Fine
Cotton Chenille.
Note: All yarns are used doubled
throughout.

A. Donegal Rainforest (489) 750[800,850]g;
B. Fine Chenille Lacquer (388) 75g;
C. Fine Chenille Willow (395) 75g;
D. Fine Chenillle Privet (394) 25g.

Pair each 3¾mm (US5) and 4½mm (US7)
needles. 1 Cable needle. 2 Stitch holders.
1 Darning needle.

TENSION (GAUGE)
21 sts and 31 rows to 10cm (4in),
measured over main pattern, using 4½mm
(US7) needles. To work main pattern, see
STITCHES below.

STITCHES
Main Pattern: Worked on sides of back
and front, and sleeves, as follows:- **Row 1
(right side):** Purl. **Row 2:** Knit. **Row 3:**
P2, * k2, p2; rep from *. **Row 4:** K2, * p2,
k2; rep from *. Rep these 4 rows. **Chart
Patterns:** Odd numbered rows are right
side, and even numbered rows are wrong
side. Colour sections are worked in st. st.
using separate lengths of doubled chenille
yarn for each area. The doubled Donegal is
stranded across the coloured areas. The
cabled stitches are worked in st. st. on a
reverse st. st. background, as indicated on
chart. **Note:** The stitch number in the
cabled panels changes at the beginning
and end of each interlaced cable. This is
indicated on the charts.

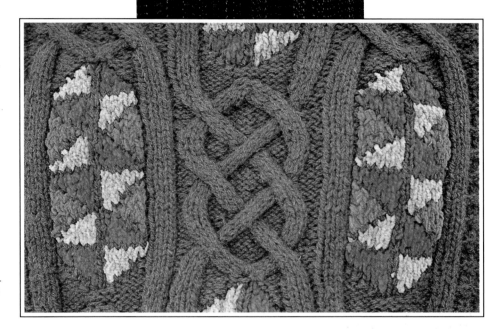

*The use of a coloured geometric motif within a knotwork pattern is a
recurrent theme in many illuminated manuscripts. The Book of Durrow, now
in Trinity College, Dublin, with its bold knotwork in black, gold, red and
green, inspired both my choice of colours and use of knotwork in this design. I
have used a panel based on these ideas for the centre back and front of this
sweater, then I highlighted the ribbed borders with stripes in the same bright
colours.*

BACK
** With 3¾mm (US5) needles and yarn B,
cast on 108[112,120] sts. K2, p2 rib for 1
row. Break off B and with C, rib 1 row.
Break off C and with A, continue until rib
measures 6.5cm 2½in from cast on edge.

Next row – Increase
Rib 6[8,4]; * m1, rib 8[6,7]; rep from * to
the last 6[8,4] sts; m1, rib 6[8,4].
121[129,137] sts.
Change to 4½mm (US7) needles and set
the patt, beg at row 1, as follows:-
Work main patt over first 30[34,38] sts;
work chart A over the next 61 sts (extra

sts are made at the centre of chart); work
main patt over the rem 30[34,38] sts.
Continue as set and work the 38 rows of
chart A, then work the 38 rows of chart B
over the centre 61 sts (extra sts are made
at the centre of cables). Alternate charts A
and B throughout, and continue as set
until back measures 40[40.5,41.5]cm
15¾[16,16¼]in from beg, with right side
facing for next row.

Shape Armholes
Keeping continuity of patt, cast off 3 sts at
beg of next 2 rows, 2 sts at beg of next 2
rows, then dec 1 st at each end of next and

CHART A

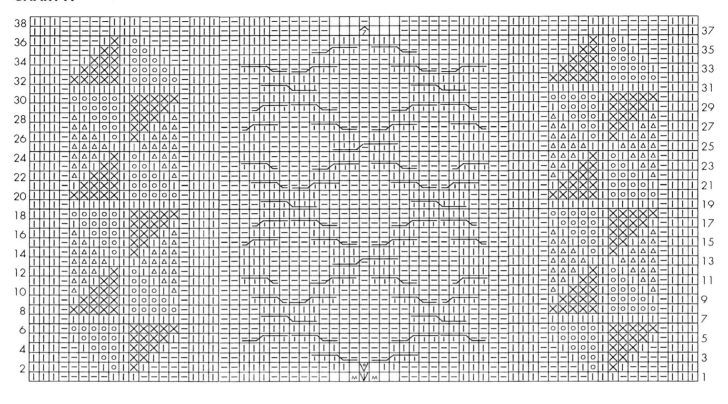

foll 2 alt rows. 22[26,30] main patt sts rem at each side. *** Continue as set until 158[164,170] rows of chart patts have been worked in total, ending with row 6[12,18] inclusive of chart A.

Shape Shoulders and Neck
Cast off 9[10,11] sts; keeping continuity, patt the next 24[26,28] sts; place the next

43[45,47] sts on a holder; leave the rem sts on a spare needle. Turn and keeping continuity as far as possible, complete right shoulder as follows:-

Row 1: Cast off 3 sts; patt to end. **Row 2**: Cast off 9[10,11] sts; patt to end. **Row 3**: Cast off 3 sts; patt to end. Cast off the rem 10[11,12] sts.

With right side facing, rejoin yarns to the sts on spare needle and keeping continuity, patt to end. **Next row**: Cast off 9[10,11] sts; patt to end. Complete shoulder as right, from row 1.

FRONT
As back from ** to ***. Continue in patts as set, until 140[144,148] chart patt rows

CHART B

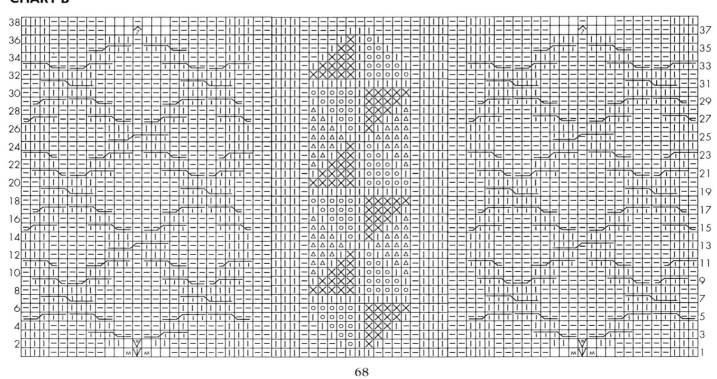

Even in retreat this sweater is stunning. The highly textured and brightly decorated cable panels occur on the back of the garment as well as the front.

have been worked in total, ending with row 26[30,34] inclusive of chart B.

Shape Neck
Patt 46[50,54] sts; place the next 25 sts on a holder; leave the rem sts on a spare needle. Turn, and keeping continuity of patt as far as possible, and remembering to reduce sts after cable as shown on chart,

KEY

☐ = no stitch

Ⅱ = k on RS rows and p on WS rows, with yarn A

⊟ = p on RS rows and k on WS rows, with yarn A

◯ = k on RS rows and p on WS rows, with yarn B

☒ = k on RS rows and p on WS rows, with yarn C

△ = k on RS rows and p on WS rows, with yarn D

Ⅳ = (k1b, k1) in one st, then insert left hand needle point behind the vertical strand that runs down from between the two sts just made and k into this strand, making the third st of the group

Ⅴ = (p1, yo, p1) into one st, making 3 sts in the group

Ⅿ = make one st by picking up strand between last st worked and next st and k into back of strand

⤒ = slip decrease 7 sts together thus: sl 4 knitwise, one at a time, with yarn at back, drop yarn then *pass the 2nd st on right hand needle over the first (centre) st: sl the centre st back to left hand needle and pass the next st on left hand needle over it*; sl the centre st back to right hand needle and rep from * to * twice more: p the centre st

⊟▱▯▯▯ = put the first st on cn and hold at back: k the next 3 sts, then p the st from cn

▯▯▯◺⊟ = put the first 3 sts on cn and hold at front: p the next st, then k the 3 sts from cn

⊟⊟◿▯▯▯ = put the first 2 sts on cn and hold at back: k the next 3 sts, then p the 2 sts from cn

▯▯▯◺⊟⊟ = put the first 3 sts on cn and hold at front: p the next 2 sts, then k the 3 sts from cn

▯▯▯◺▯▯▯ = put the first 3 sts on cn and hold at front: k the next 3 sts, then k the 3 sts from cn

▯▯▯▯◿▯▯▯ = put the first 4 sts on cn and hold at back: k the next 3 sts, sl the p st from cn back onto left hand needle and p this st, then k the rem 3 sts from cn

'Durrow' is a perfect example of combining techniques to maximize the effect. Interlacing cable panels enclose areas of bright Fair Isle colourwork, while the main fabric is a simple variation of textured rib.

shape left neck and shoulder as follows:-
Dec 1 st at neck edge of next 6 rows, then on every foll alt row 5[6,7] times. Patt 1 row straight. **Next row**: With right side facing, cast off 9[10,11] sts; patt to the last 2 sts; k2tog. Patt 1 row straight. Cast off 9[10,11] sts at beg of next row and patt to end. Patt 1 row straight. Cast off the rem 10[11,12] sts.

With right side facing, rejoin yarns to sts on spare needle, and keeping continuity, patt to end. Shape right neck and shoulder as left, but beg shoulder shaping on wrong side row.

SLEEVES
With 3¼mm (US5) needles and yarn B, cast on 44[48,52] sts and work rib as back and front for 6.5cm 2½in.
Next row – Increase
Rib 4[1,3]; * m1, rib 4[5,5]; rep from * to the last 4[2,4] sts; m1, rib 4[2,4].
54[58,62] sts.

Change to 4½mm (US7) needles and work all sts in main patt. Increase 1 st at each end of 3rd and every foll 5th row until

there are 100[106,110] sts, working all increased sts into patt. Continue straight in patt until sleeve measures 47[48,49]cm 18½[19,19¼]in from cast on edge.

Shape Top
Keeping continuity of patt, cast off 5 sts at beg of next 10 rows. Patt 1 row straight, then cast off the rem 50[56,60] sts.

FINISHING
Join back and front at left shoulder seam.

COLLAR
With right side facing, 3¾mm (US5) needles and yarn A, beg at right back neck and pick up sts for collar as follows:-
First size: Knit up 6 sts to back neck holder; from holder, k2tog, k9, (k2tog) 3 times, k9, (k2tog) 3 times, k9, k2tog; knit up 24 sts evenly to front neck holder; pick up and k 25 sts from holder; knit up 18 sts evenly to top right front. 108 sts.

Second size: Knit up 6 sts to back neck holder; from holder, k2tog, k17, sl dec next 7 sts tog as worked on chart, k17,

k2tog; knit up 25 sts evenly to front neck holder; pick up and k 25 sts from holder; knit up 19 sts evenly to top right front. 112 sts.

Third size: Knit up 6 sts to back neck holder; from holder, k2tog, k11, (k2tog) 3 times, k9, (k2tog) 3 times, k11, k2tog; knit up 26 sts evenly to front neck holder; pick up and k 25 sts from front neck holder, knit up 20 sts evenly to top right front. 116 sts.

All sizes: K2, p2 rib for 6.5cm 2½in. Break off yarn A and with C, rib 1 row. Break off yarn C and with B, rib 1 row. With B, cast off evenly, knitwise.

Join right shoulder and collar seam. Turn collar in half to outside and with single strand of A, catch-stitch last row of collar rib, worked in A, to collar pick up line. Sew sleeve tops into armholes. Press seams lightly on wrong side, omitting collar rib. Join side and sleeve seams. Press seams lightly on wrong side, omitting ribs.

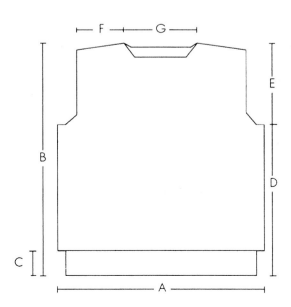

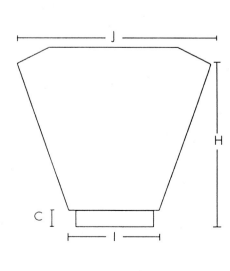

A = 54.5 [58.5, 62.5]cm
B = 64 [66, 68]cm
C = 6.5cm
D = 40 [40.5, 41.5]cm
E = 24 [25.5, 26.5]cm
F = 14.5 [16.5, 18]cm
G = 22 [23, 24]cm
H = 47 [48, 49]cm
I = 26 [28, 30]cm
J = 48 [51, 53]cm

A = 21½ [23, 24½]in
B = 25½ [26, 26¾]in
C = 2½in
D = 15¾ [16, 16¼]in
E = 9½ [10, 10½]in
F = 5¾ [6½, 7]in
G = 8¾ [9, 9½]in
H = 18½ [19, 19¼]in
I = 10¼ [11, 11¾]in
J = 19 [20, 21]in

TARA
SWEATER
IN CELTIC
KNOTWORK

RATING
★ ★

SIZES
To fit bust 81-86[91-97,102-107]cm
32-34[36-38,40-42]in.
Directions for larger sizes are given in
parenthesis. Where there is only one set of
figures, it applies to all sizes.

KNITTED
MEASUREMENTS
Underarm 119[132,145]cm 47[52,57]in.
Length from top of shoulder 47[50,53]cm
18½[19¾,21]in.
Sleeve length 40[4l,42.5]cm
15¾[16¼,16¾]in.

MATERIALS
Yarn: 675[700,750]g Rowan Donegal
Lambswool Tweed in shade no. 465
(Ivory), used doubled throughout.

1 Pair 5mm (US8) needles. 1 Cable needle.

TENSION (GAUGE)
19 sts and 28 rows to 10cm (4in),
measured over main pattern using 5mm
(US8) needles. To work main pattern, see
STITCHES below.

STITCHES
Main Pattern: Worked on back, sleeves,
and main part of front. **Row 1:** (right side)
K1, p1, rep to last st, k1. **Row 2:** Knit. Rep
these 2 rows. **Chart Patterns:** Odd
numbered rows are right side, and even
numbered rows are wrong side. Cabled sts
are worked in st.st. on a reverse st.st.
background, as indicated on chart. The
emblem on the front is surrounded by the
main pattern. **Note:** The st number in
Charts A and B increases at the beginning
and decreases at the end of each chart.
This is indicated on the charts.

*The modern cropped style of this sweater
makes it ideal for casual wear. It looks
stylish teamed with a waistcoat.*

BACK
* With 5mm (US8) needles and yarn
doubled, cast on 109[121,133] sts. K 4
rows. P 1 row. K 1 row. Then work the
patt from chart A, repeating the 12
(increased to 18) patt sts 9[10,11] times,
then work the last st from chart. Continue
and work all 33 rows of chart. K 5 rows,
increasing 1 st at each end of the 5th row.
111[123,135] sts. **

Work in main pattern (see STITCHES),
and continue straight until back measures
22[24,26]cm 8¾[9½,10¼]in from beg, with
right side facing for next row.

Shape Armholes
Keeping continuity of patt, cast off 3[4,4]
sts at beg of next 2 rows; 2[2,3] sts at beg
of next 2 rows; dec 1 st at each end of next
and foll 2[3,4] alt rows. 95[103,111] sts
rem. Continue straight in main patt until
armholes measure 25[26,27]cm
9¾[10¼,10¾]in, with right side facing for
next row.

Shape Neck and Shoulders
Keeping continuity of patt, cast off 8[9,10]
sts; patt 21[23,25] sts including st used to
cast off; cast off the next 37[39,41] sts;
patt to end of row. Keeping continuity of
patt, shape right shoulder as follows:-
Row 1: Cast off 8[9,10] sts; patt to end.
Row 2: Cast off 2 sts; patt to end. **Row 3:**
Cast off 9[10,11] sts; patt to the last 2 sts ;
k2tog. Patt 1 row straight. Cast off the rem
9[10,11] sts.

With wrong side facing, rejoin yarn to sts
of left shoulder and complete as right
shoulder, working from row 2.

FRONT
As back from * to **. Continue in main
patt until front measures
20.5[22.5,24.5]cm 8[8¾,9½]in from beg,
with right side facing for next row.
Position chart B emblem as follows:-
Keeping continuity , work main pattern
over the next 55[61,67] sts; work row 1
of chart B over the next st; work main patt
over the rem sts. Continue as set and work
the 47 rows of chart B, and work the sts at
each side in main patt. AT THE SAME
TIME, when front corresponds in length
with back at beg of armholes, shape

*I wanted to bring the idea of
knotwork as a symbol of continuity
to the fore in a single emblem on the
chest of this sweater. The highly
sculptured quality of the emblem is
accentuated by the neatly textured
background, and makes it easy to
trace the unbroken line. A wide
band of knotwork motifs decorates
the lower edge of the body and
sleeves, while the neckband is an
unusual double row of plaited
cables.*

CHART A

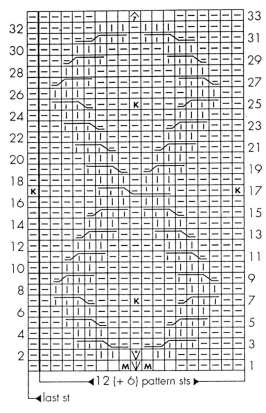

◀12 (+ 6) pattern sts ▶

└◀last st

CHART C

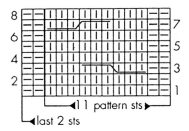

◀11 pattern sts▶

└◀last 2 sts

KEY

☐ = no stitch

Ⅰ = k on RS rows and p on WS rows

⊟ = p on RS rows and k on WS rows

Ⅴ = (k1b, k1) in one st, then insert left hand needle point behind the vertical strand that runs down between the 2 sts just made and k into this strand making the 3rd st of the group

Ⅴ = (p1, yo, p1) into one st, making 3 sts in the group

Ⅿ = make one st by picking up strand between last st worked and next st, and k into back of strand

Ⅺ = make knot thus: (k1b, k1) twice into one st, making 4 sts, then pass the first 3 sts made over the last st made

⑦ = slip decrease 7 sts together thus: sl 4 knitwise, one at a time, with yarn at back, drop yarn then *pass the 2nd st on right hand needle over the first (centre) st: sl the centre st back to left hand needle and pass the next st on left hand needle over it*; sl the centre st back to right hand needle and rep from * to * twice more: p the centre st

= put the first st on cn and hold at back: k the next 3 sts, then p the st from cn

= put the first 3 sts on cn and hold at front: p the next st, then k the 3 sts from cn

= put the first 3 sts on cn and hold at front: k the next st, then k 3 sts from cn

= put the first st on cn and hold at back: k the next 3 sts, then k the st from cn

= put the first 2 sts on cn and hold at back: k the next 3 sts, then p the 2 sts from cn

= put the first 3 sts on cn and hold at front: p the next 2 sts, then k the 3 sts from cn

= put the first 3 sts on cn and hold at front: k1, p1, then k the 3 sts from cn

= put the first 2 sts on cn and hold at back: k the next 3 sts, then p1, k1 from cn

= put the first 3 sts on cn and hold at front: p1, k1, then k the 3 sts from cn

= put the first 2 sts on cn and hold at back: k the next 3 sts, then k1, p1 from cn

= put the first 3 sts on cn and hold at back: k the next 3 sts, then k the 3 sts from cn

= put the first 3 sts on cn and hold at front: k the next 3 sts, then k the 3 sts from cn

= put the first 3 sts on cn and hold at front: p the next 3 sts, then k the 3 sts from cn

= put the first 3 sts on cn and hold at back: k the next 3 sts, then p the 3 sts from cn

= put the first 3 sts on cn and hold at back: k the next 3 sts, then p1, k1, p1 from cn

= put the first 3 sts on cn and hold at front: p1, k1, p1, then k the 3 sts from cn

= put the first 4 sts on cn and hold at back: k the next 3 sts, sl the p st from cn back onto left hand needle and p this st, then k rem 3 sts from cn

= put the first 4 sts on cn and hold at front: k the next 3 sts, sl the p st from cn back onto left hand needle and p this st, then k rem 3 sts from cn

CHART B

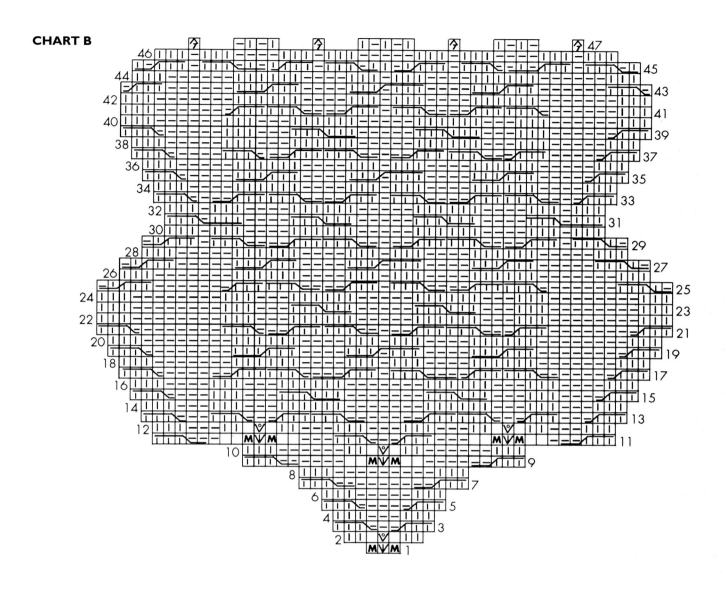

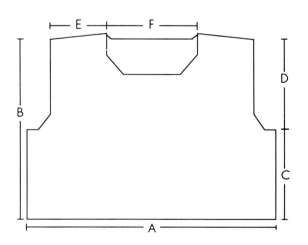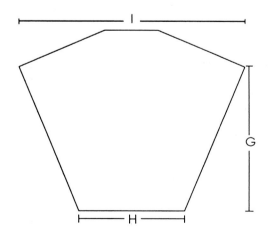

A = 59.5 [66, 72.5]cm   23½ [26, 28½]in
B = 47 [50, 52]cm   18½ [19¾, 21]in
C = 22 [24, 26]cm   8¾ [9½, 10¼]in
D = 25 [26, 27]cm   9¾ [10¼, 10¾]in
E = 14 [15, 17]cm   5½ [6, 6¾]in

F = 23 [24, 25]cm   9 [9½, 9¾]in
G = 40 [41, 42.5]cm   15¾ [16¼, 16¾]in
H = 27 [28, 30.5]cm   10½ [11, 12]in
I = 56 [59.5, 61.5]cm   22 [23½, 24¼]in

Worked entirely in a creamy woollen yarn, the knotwork textures here are very prominent. The main emblem is a clever mass of cables with no broken lines.

previous side, except begin shoulder shaping with wrong side facing.

SLEEVES

With yarn doubled, cast on 49[53,57] sts. K 4 rows. P 1 row. K 1 row. Then work chart A as follows:-
P0[2,4]; rep the 12 (increased to 18) patt sts 4 times; work the last st from chart; p0[2,4]. Continue as set and work all 33 rows of chart. Work the extra sts on second and third sizes in reverse st.st. On all sizes, increase 1 st at each end of 3rd and every foll 6th row, working all increased sts in reverse st.st. K 5 rows, increasing 1 st at each end of 5th row. Continue in main patt and increase 1 st at each end of every 3rd row until there are 105[111,115] sts, working all increased sts into main patt. Continue straight in patt until sleeve measures 40[41,42.5]cm 15¾[16¼, 16¾]in from beg.

Shape Top
Keeping continuity of patt, cast off 5 sts at beg of next 12[14,16] rows. Patt 1 row straight. Cast off the rem 45[41,35] sts.

FINISHING
Join back and front at shoulder seams. Press seams lightly on wrong side.

COLLAR
With yarn doubled, cast on 35 sts. Work the patt from chart C, repeating the 11 patt sts 3 times, then work the last 2 sts. Rep the 8 patt rows until collar measures 53[55,57]cm 21[21¾, 22½]in. Cast off all sts.
With right sides of collar and body facing each other, place cast on end of collar at left shoulder seam. Pin and stitch collar around neckline, easing neckline evenly along back neck and around front neck, so that cast off end meets cast on end at shoulder seam. Sew ends of collar together. Turn collar in half to the inside and slip stitch in position.

Fold sleeves in half lengthwise and mark centre top. Place centre top of sleeve at shoulder seam and sew sleeves into armholes. Press seams lightly on wrong side. Sew up side and sleeve seams. Press seams lightly on wrong side.

armholes as back. Continue straight in main patt at armholes and then on all sts on completion of chart B, until armholes measure 18[18.5,19]cm 7[7¼,7½]in, with right side facing for next row.

Shape Front Neck
Keeping continuity, patt 40[43,46] sts; leave the rem sts on a spare needle. Shape left side as follows :-
Keeping continuity of patt, cast off 2 sts at beg of next and foll alt row. Dec 1 st at neck edge of next 4 rows. Patt 1 row straight, then dec 1 st at neck edge of next and foll 5 alt rows. 26[29,32] sts rem.

Continue straight in patt until armhole corresponds in length with back armhole, with right side facing for next row.

Shape Shoulder
Keeping continuity of patt, cast off 8[9,10] sts at beg of next row. Patt 1 row straight. Cast off 9[10,11] sts at beg of next row. Patt 1 row straight. Cast off the rem 9[10,11] sts.

With right side facing, rejoin yarn and cast off the first 15[17,19] sts; keeping continuity, patt to end. Patt 1 row straight, then complete neck and shoulder as

CASHEL
CHILD'S SWEATER
IN CELTIC KNOTWORK

RATING

For the child's version of Tara, I decided to use an easier knotwork emblem and border pattern. These designs are off-set against a simple textured two-row background, with one row worked in single rib and the other knitted. A lighter effect has been achieved by using a single strand of tweed yarn, rather than the double thickness of Tara.

SIZES
To fit age 6-7[8-9,10-11] years. Directions for larger sizes are given in parenthesis. Where there is only one set of figures, it applies to all sizes.

KNITTED MEASUREMENTS
Underarm 76[85,94]cm 30[33½,37]in. Length from top of shoulder 38[42,46]cm 15[16½,18]in. Sleeve length 31[33,36]cm 12[13,14]in.

MATERIALS
Yarn: 6[7,8] 50g balls Rowan Lambswool Tweed in shade no. 182 (Dark Emerald).

1 Pair 4mm (US6) needles. 1 Cable needle. Stitch markers. 1 Darner.

TENSION (GAUGE)
12 sts and 18 rows to 5cm (2in), measured over main pattern (see STITCHES), using 4mm (US6) needles.

STITCHES
Main Pattern: Worked on back, sleeves, and main part of front as follows:-
First and Third Sizes Only: Row 1: (right side) K1, p1; rep to the last st; k1.
Row 2: Knit. Rep these 2 rows.

Second Size Only: Row 1: (right side) P1, k1; rep to the last st; p1. **Row 2**: Knit. Rep these 2 rows.

Chart Patterns: Odd numbered rows are right side, and even numbered rows are wrong side. The cabled sts are worked in st.st. on a reverse st.st. background, as indicated on charts. The chart B emblem is surrounded by the main pattern. **Note**: The st number in charts A and B increases at the beginning and decreases at the end as indicated on the charts.

BACK
* With 4mm (US6) needles, cast on 91[101,111] sts. K 4 rows. Work the patt from chart A, repeating the 10 (increased to 14) patt sts 9[10,11] times, then work the last st from chart. Work all 18 rows of chart, ending with right side facing for next row. **
Continue straight in main patt (see STITCHES) until back measures

20[22.5,24.5]cm 8[8¾,9½]in from beg. Place a marker at each end of row and continue straight in patt until back measures 38[42,46]cm 15[16½,18]in, ending with right side facing for next row.

Shape Shoulders
Keeping continuity of patt, cast off 8[10,11] sts at beg of next 2 rows. Cast off 9[10,11] sts at beg of next 2 rows. Cast off 9[10,12] sts at beg of next 2 rows. Cast off the rem 39[41,43] sts.

FRONT
As back from * to **. Continue straight in main patt until front measures 16[18,21]cm 6¼[7,8¼]in from beg, with right side facing for next row. Position chart B emblem as follows:-
Keeping continuity, work main patt over

the first 38[43,48] sts; work row 1 of chart B over the next 15 sts, increasing as indicated on chart; work main patt over the rem 38[43,48] sts. Continue as set and work the 37 rows of chart B and work the main patt over the sts at each side. On completion of chart B, keep continuity and resume working main patt over all sts until front measures 33[36,40]cm 13[14¼,15¾]in from beg, with right side facing for next row.

Shape Neck
Keeping continuity, patt 37[41,45] sts; leave the rem sts on a spare needle. Turn and shape left side as follows:-
Keeping continuity of patt, dec 1 st at neck edge of next 6 rows. Patt 1 row straight, then dec 1 st at neck edge of next and foll alt rows 5 times in all. 26[30,34] sts rem.

CHART A

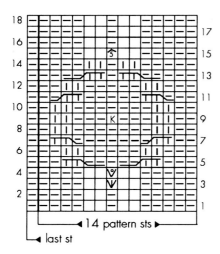

◀ 14 pattern sts ▶

◀ last st

CHART C

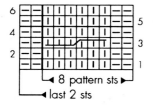

◀ 8 pattern sts ▶

◀ last 2 sts

CHART B

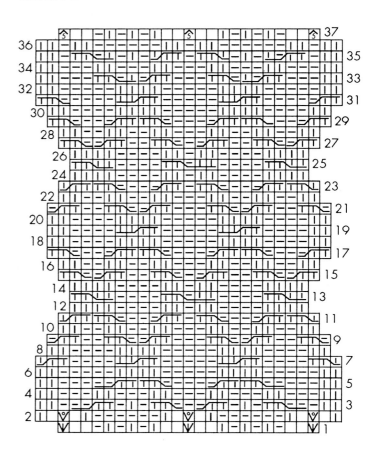

KEY

□ = no stitch

Ⅰ = k on RS rows and p on WS rows

⊟ = p on RS rows and k on WS rows

Ⅴ = (k1b, k1) in one st, then insert left hand needle point behind the vertical strand that runs down between the 2 sts just made and k into this strand making the 3rd st of the group

Ⅴ = (p1, yo, p1) into one st, making 3 sts in the group

K = make knot thus: (k1b, k1) twice in one st, making 4 sts, then pass the first 3 sts over the last one made

Ⓢ = slip decrease 5 sts together thus: sl 3 knitwise, one at a time, with yarn at back, drop yarn then *pass the 2nd st on right hand needle over the first (centre) st: sl the centre st back to left hand needle and pass the next st on left hand needle over it*; sl the centre st back to right hand needle and rep from * to * once more: p the centre st

= put the first st on cn and hold at back: k the next 2 sts, then p the st from cn

= put the first 2 sts on cn and hold at front: p the next st, then k the 2 sts from cn

= put the first 2 sts on cn and hold at front: k the next st, then k the 2 sts from cn

= put the first st on cn and hold at back: k the next 2 sts, then k the st from cn

= put the first 2 sts on cn and hold at back: k the next 2 sts, then p the 2 sts from cn

= put the first 2 sts on cn and hold at front: p the next 2 sts, then k the 2 sts from cn

= put the first 2 sts on cn and hold at back: k the next 2 sts, then k the 2 sts from cn

= put the first 2 sts on cn and

hold at front: k the next 2 sts, then k the 2 sts from cn

= put the first 2 sts on cn and hold at back: k the next 2 sts, then p1, k1 from cn

= put the first 2 sts on cn and hold at front: k1, p1, then k the 2 sts from cn

= put the first 3 sts on cn and hold at front: k the next 2 sts, sl the p st from cn back onto left hand needle and p it, then k the 2 sts from cn

= put the first 3 sts on cn and hold at back: k the next 3 sts, then k the 3 sts from cn

'Cashel' echoes the cropped shape and style of Tara, but the details are scaled down and simplified for a child.

If necessary, continue straight in patt until front corresponds in length with back at beg of shoulder shaping, with right side facing for next row.

Shape Shoulder
Keeping continuity of patt, cast off

8[10,11] sts at beg of next row. Cast off 9[10,11] sts at beg of next alt row. Cast off 9[10,12] sts at beg of next alt row. With right side facing, rejoin yarn to sts on spare needle and cast off the first 17[19,21] sts; patt to end of row. Then complete as previous side, except beg

shoulder shaping with wrong side facing. Place a marker at each side of front to correspond with those on back.

SLEEVES
With 4mm (US6) needles, cast on 45[49,53] sts. K 4 rows. Work chart A as follows:-
P2[4,1]; rep the 10 (increased to 14) patt sts 4[4,5] times; patt the last st of chart; p2[4,1]. Continue as set and work all 18 rows of chart A, working the extra sts at each side in reverse st.st. Then continue in main patt, increasing 1 st at each end of 3rd and every foll 4th row until there are 85[93,103] sts. Work all increased sts into main patt. Continue straight in patt until sleeve measures 31[33,36]cm 12[13,14]in from beg. Cast off all sts.

FINISHING
Do not press pieces. Join back and front at shoulder seams. Press seams lightly on wrong side.

COLLAR
With 4mm (US6) needles, cast on 26 sts. Work the patt from chart C, repeating the 8 patt sts 3 times, then work the last 2 sts. Rep the 6 patt rows until collar measures 46[48,50]cm 18[18¾, 19½]in. Cast off all sts. With right side of collar and body facing each other, place the cast on end of collar at right shoulder seam. Pin, then stitch collar along back neck and around front neck evenly, so that cast on end of collar meets cast on end at shoulder seam. Sew ends of collar together. Turn collar in half to the inside and slip stitch in position. Place centre top of sleeve at shoulder seam and sew sleeves to body between markers. Press seams lightly on wrong side. Sew up side and sleeve seams, then press seams lightly on wrong side.

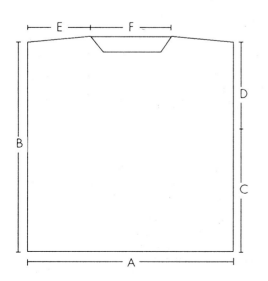

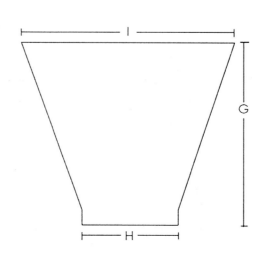

A = 38 [42.5, 47]cm
B = 38 [42, 46]cm
C = 20 [22.5, 24.5]cm
D = 18 [19.5, 21.5]cm
E = 10.5 [12.5, 14.5]cm
F = 17 [17.5, 18]cm
G = 31 [33, 36]cm
H = 19 [20.5, 22.5]cm
I = 36 [39, 43]cm

A = 15 [16¾, 18½]in
B = 15 [16½, 18]in
C = 8 [8¾, 9½]in
D = 7 [7¾, 8¾]in
E = 4¼ [5, 5¾]in
F = 6½ [6¾, 7]in
G = 12 [13, 14]in
H = 7½ [8¼, 8¾]in
I = 14 [15½, 17]in

IONA
SWEATER
IN CELTIC KNOTWORK

RATING

★ ★

SIZES

To fit bust/chest 86-91[97-102,107-112]cm 34-36[38-40,42-44]in.
Directions for larger sizes are given in parenthesis. Where there is only one set of figures, it applies to all sizes.

KNITTED MEASUREMENTS

Underarm 126[130,136]cm 49½[51½,53½]in.
Length from top of shoulder 60[62.5,65]cm 23½[24½, 25½]in.
Sleeve length 45.5[47,48]cm 18[18½,19]in.

MATERIALS

Yarn: Rowan Cotton Chenille Chunky Weight.

Driftwood (352) 700[700,800]g; Forest Green (362) 100[200,200]g.

1 Pair each 3¾mm (US5), 4½mm (US7) and 5mm (US8) needles. 1 40cm (16in) long circular or set of double-pointed 5mm (US8) needles. 1 Cable needle. 2 Stitch holders. 4 Stitch markers.

TENSION (GAUGE)

16 sts and 24 rows to 10cm (4in), measured over reverse st.st., using 4½mm (US7) needles.

STITCHES

Reverse st.st.: P right side rows and k wrong side rows.**Chart patterns**: Odd numbered rows are right side, and even numbered rows are wrong side. The cabled sts are worked in st.st. on a reverse st.st. background, as indicated on chart. **Note**: The st number increases at the beginning and decreases at the end of both charts. This is indicated on the charts.

BACK

* With 3¾mm (US5) needles and Forest Green, cast on 98[102,106] sts and k 2 rows. Change to 5mm (US8) needles, join in Driftwood and work check border as follows :-
Row 1 (right side): K2 Forest Green, k2 Driftwood; rep to the last 2 sts; k2 Forest Green. **Row 2**: P2 Forest Green, p2 Driftwood; rep to last 2 sts; p2 Forest

A soft chunky chenille yarn in a lovely heathery tone was the starting point of this design; it reminded me of the moors in my native countryside. This time I have worked a single knotwork emblem on the back and front of a sweater, with a simplified version on the sleeves. The two-tone checked pattern on the borders echoes those used to frame more elaborate designs in the ancient manuscripts.

Green. **Row 3**: K2 Driftwood, k2 Forest Green; rep to the last 2 sts; k2 Driftwood. **Row 4**: P2 Driftwood, p2 Forest Green; rep to the last 2 sts; p2 Driftwood. Rep these 4 rows 3 more times, then work rows 1 and 2 once more, working 18 rows in total. Break off Driftwood.
Change to 4½mm (US7) needles and with Forest Green, k 4 rows. Break off Forest Green. With Driftwood k 1 row, decreasing 1 st at centre. 97[101,105] sts. Work reverse st.st. for 21 rows, ending with right side facing for next row. Position chart A emblem as follows :- P47[49,51]; work row 1 of chart over the next 3 sts; p47[49,51]. Continue as set and work all 97 rows of chart A. AT THE SAME TIME, when back measures 33[35,36.5]cm 13[13¾,14¼]in, place a marker at each end of row.** On completion of chart, continue straight in reverse st.st. for a further 35[41,47] rows, ending with right side facing for next row.

Shape Back Neck and Shoulders

Cast off 11[11,12]; p24[25,26]; place the next 27[29,29] sts on a holder for centre back neck; leave the rem sts on a spare needle. Turn and complete right shoulder as follows :-
Row 1: K2tog, k22[23,24]. **Row 2**: Cast off 11[11,12]; p12[13,13]. **Row 3**: K2tog, k10[11,11]. Cast off the rem 11[12,12] sts.

With right side facing, rejoin yarn and p the 35[36,38] sts from spare needle and complete the left shoulder as follows:-
Row 1: Cast off 11[11,12]; k22[23,24]; k2tog. **Row 2**: P23[24,25]. **Row 3**: Cast off 11[11,12]; k10[11,11]; k2tog. **Row 4**: P11[12,12]. Cast off the rem 11[12,12] sts.

FRONT

As back from * to **. On completion of chart, continue straight in reverse st.st. for a further 23[27,31] rows, ending with right side facing for next row.

Shape Front Neck

P43[45,47]; place the next 11 sts on a holder for centre front neck; leave the rem sts on a spare needle. Working the first 43[45,47] sts, shape left side of neck by dec 1 st at neck edge of next 10[11,11] rows. Continue straight until left front

Velvety chenille yarn makes an exquisite fabric for this elaborate arrangement of interlacing cables which stand out in sharp relief against a simple background.

Change to 4½mm (US7) needles, join in Driftwood, and work 18 rows in check patt as back. **Note**: For second size only, omit the last 2 sts of check pattern. Break off Driftwood, and with Forest Green, k 4 rows. Break off Forest Green. With Driftwood, increase as follows:-
K2[3,1]; * m1, k5[5,6]; rep from * to the last 2[3,1] sts; m1, k2[3,1]. 41[43,45] sts.

Working in reverse st.st., increase 1 st at each end of every 4th row, and work 5[9,13] rows in total, ending with right side facing for next row. Position chart B emblem as follows:-
P20[22,24]; work row 1 of chart B over the next 3 sts; p20[22,24]. Continue as set, increasing 1 st at each end of every 4th row, and work all 69 rows of chart. Then continue in reverse st.st., increasing as set until there are 81[85,89] sts. Continue straight until sleeve measures 45.5[47,48]cm 18[18½,19]in from beg. Cast off all sts.

FINISHING
Do not press pieces. Join back and front at shoulder seams. Press seams lightly on wrong side. Place centre of sleeves at shoulder seams and sew in sleeves between markers. Press seams lightly on wrong side. Sew up side and sleeve seams and press lightly on wrong side.

COLLAR
With right side facing, 5mm (US8) double-pointed or circular needles and Driftwood, pick up and k the 27[29,29] sts from back neck holder; knit up 21[22,24] sts to front neck holder; pick up and k the 11 sts from holder; knit up 21[22,24] sts to complete rnd. 80[84,88] sts. Place a marker at beg of rnd, and with Forest Green, k 1 rnd; p 1 rnd. Rep these last 2 rnds once again. Work check border as follows:-
Rnds 1 and, 2: K2 Driftwood, k2 Forest Green; rep to end of rnd.
Rnds 3 and 4: K2 Forest Green, k2 Driftwood; rep to end of rnd.
Continue in this manner, working 10 rnds of check border patt in total. Break off Driftwood and with Forest Green, k 1 rnd; p 1 rnd; k 1 rnd. Cast off evenly, purlwise. Darn in loose ends.

Styled for comfort, 'Iona' is the perfect sweater for relaxing countryside pursuits.

matches back in length at beg of shoulder shaping, with right side facing for next row. Shape shoulder by casting off 11[11,12] sts at beg of next and foll alt row. K 1 row, then cast off the rem 11[12,12] sts.

With right side facing, rejoin yarn and p the 43[45,47] sts from spare needle. Shape right neck and shoulder as left, reversing all shapings.

SLEEVES
With 3¾mm (US5) needles and Forest Green, cast on 34[36,38] sts and k 2 rows.

CHART A

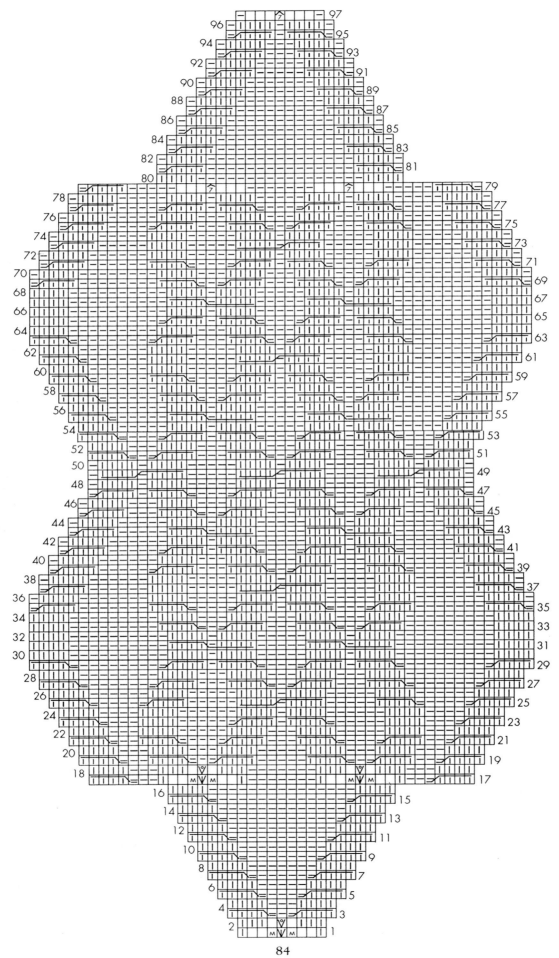

CHART B

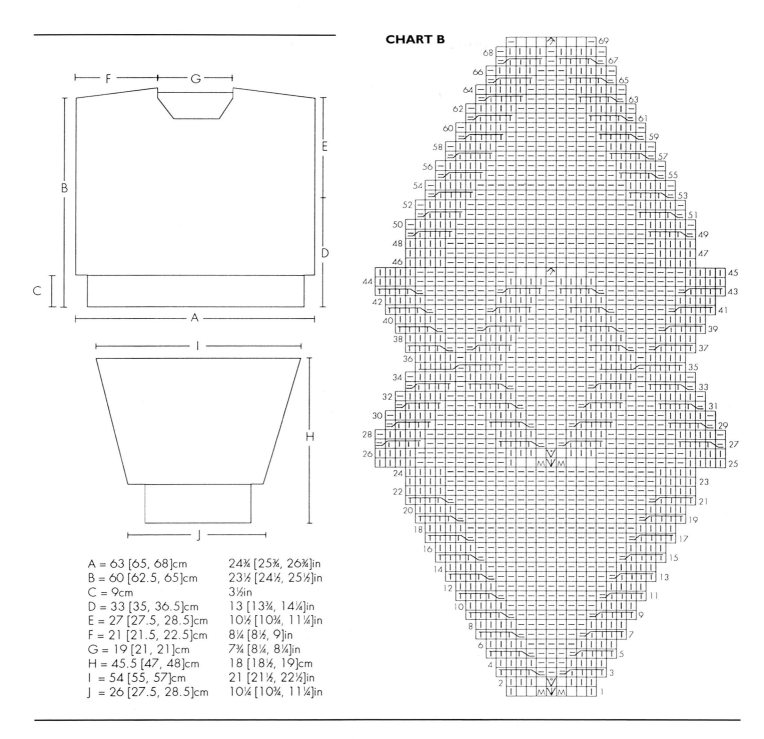

A = 63 [65, 68]cm   24¾ [25¾, 26¾]in
B = 60 [62.5, 65]cm   23½ [24½, 25½]in
C = 9cm   3½in
D = 33 [35, 36.5]cm   13 [13¾, 14¼]in
E = 27 [27.5, 28.5]cm   10½ [10¾, 11¼]in
F = 21 [21.5, 22.5]cm   8¼ [8½, 9]in
G = 19 [21, 21]cm   7¾ [8¼, 8¼]in
H = 45.5 [47, 48]cm   18 [18½, 19]cm
I = 54 [55, 57]cm   21 [21½, 22½]in
J = 26 [27.5, 28.5]cm   10¼ [10¾, 11¼]in

KEY

☐ = no stitch

Ⅰ = k on RS rows and p on WS rows

⊟ = p on RS rows and k on WS rows

Ⓥ = (k1b, k1) in one st, then insert left hand needle point behind the vertical strand that runs down between the 2 sts just made and k into this strand, making the third st of the group

Ⓥ = (p1, yo, p1) into one st, making 3 sts in the group

Ⓜ = make one st by picking up the strand between last st worked and next st, and k into the back of strand

↗ = slip decrease 7 sts together thus: sl 4 knitwise, one at a time, with yarn at back, drop yarn then, *pass the 2nd st on right hand needle over the first (centre) st: sl the centre st back to left hand needle and pass the next st on left hand needle over it;* sl the centre st back to right hand needle and rep from * to * twice more: p the centre st

⊟╱ⅠⅠⅠⅠⅠ = put the first st on cn and hold at back: k the next 4 sts, then p the st from cn

ⅠⅠⅠⅠⅠ╲⊟ = put the first 4 sts on cn and hold at front: p the next st, then k the 4 sts from cn

ⅠⅠⅠⅠⅠⅤ╱ⅠⅠⅠⅠ = put the first 5 sts on cn and hold at back: k the next 4 sts, sl the p st from cn back onto left hand needle and p this st, then k the rem 4 sts from cn

ⅠⅠⅠⅠⅠ╲ⅤⅠⅠⅠⅠ = put the first 5 sts on cn and hold at front: k the next 4 sts, sl the p st from cn back onto left hand needle and p this st, then k the rem 4 sts from cn

GALWAY
CHILD'S SWEATER
IN CELTIC KNOTWORK

RATING

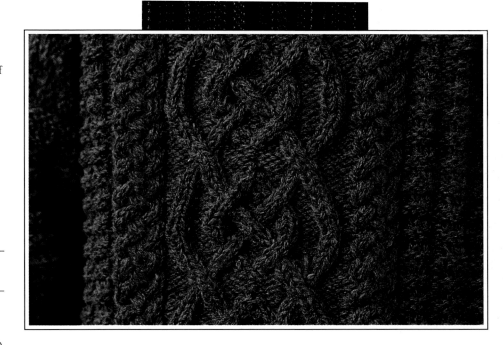

I like my designs to fit as many sizes as possible. Once I am working on a theme, then I will often make a slightly different version to fit a child. The centre sleeve panel of Kilronan is the perfect size and scale for the main panel of this child's sweater. The style is suitably casual in a tweed yarn worked double for the toughest wear, with just a touch of chenille in the check patterned borders.

SIZES
To fit age 6-7[8-9,10-11] years. Directions for larger sizes are given in parenthesis. Where there is only one set of figures, it applies to all sizes.

KNITTED MEASUREMENTS
Underarm 80[88,94]cm 31½[34½,37]in. Length from top of shoulder 42.5[46,50]cm 16¾[18, 19¾]in. Sleeve length 34.5[37,41]cm 13½[14½,16]in.

MATERIALS
Yarn: Rowan Donegal Lambswool Tweed; Fine Cotton Chenille.

A. Pickle Donegal Tweed (483) 450[500,550]g; **B.** Lacquer Fine Chenille (388) 50g.

Note: Both yarns are used doubled throughout.

1 Pair each 3¾mm (US5) and 4½mm (US7) needles. 1 Cable needle. 2 Stitch holders. Stitch markers. 1 Darner.

TENSION (GAUGE)
22 sts and 31 rows to 10cm (4in), measured over main patt, using 4½mm (US7) needles. To work the main patt, see STITCHES below.

STITCHES
Main Patt: Worked at each side of back, front and sleeves, as follows:- **Row 1** (right side): Purl. **Row 2**: Knit. **Row 3**: P2, * k2, p2; rep from *. **Row 4**: K2, * p2, k2; rep from *. Rep these 4 rows. **Chart Patt**: Odd numbered rows are right side, and even numbered rows are wrong side. The cabled sts are worked in st.st. on a reverse st.st. background, as indicated on charts. **Note**: The stitch number in chart B increases at the beginning and decreases to the original number at the end of the panel. This is indicated on the chart.

Knitted in a double thickness of tweedy yarn with a hint of chenille in the trimming, 'Galway' makes a rugged outdoor sweater for a child.

BACK
** With 4½mm (US7) needles and 2 strands of yarn A, cast on 86[94,102] sts. Join in 2 strands of yarn B and work check border as follows:-
Row 1: (right side) * K2 A, p2 B; rep from * to the last 2 sts; k2 A. **Row 2**: * P2 A, k2 B; rep from * to the last 2 sts; p2 A. **Row 3**: * K2 B, p2 A; rep from * to the last 2 sts; k2 B. **Row 4**: * P2 B, k2 A; rep from * to the last 2 sts; p2 B. Rep these 4 rows and work 9[11,11] rows in total. Break off yarn B.

Next Row: K26[30,34]; p8; k9; m1; k9; p8; k26[30,34]. 87[95,103] sts. Beg at row 1 of all patts and set as follows:-
Work main patt over the first 26[30,34] sts; chart A over the next 8 sts; chart B over the next 19 sts, increasing as indicated; chart A over the next 8 sts; main patt over the rem 26[30,34] sts. Continue as set, repeating the 4 rows of main patt and chart A, and work the first 34 rows of chart B once only, thereafter rep row 15 through row 34. When back measures 23.5[25,27]cm 9¼[9¾,10¾]in from beg, place a marker at each side of row. ***

Continue in patts as set and work 114[114,134] rows of patts in total, ending after row 34 of chart B. Continue in main patt and chart A as set, and work row 35 through 38 of chart B over centre sts.

Second Size Only: Work a further 6 rows of main patt and chart A as set, and work reverse st.st. over the centre 19 sts.

87

CHART A

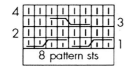

KEY

☐ = no stitch

Ⅰ = k on RS rows and p on WS rows

⊟ = p on RS rows and k on WS rows

Ⅴ = (k1b, k1) in one st, then insert left hand needle point behind the vertical strand that runs down between the 2 sts just made and k into this strand making the 3rd st of the group

Ⅴ = (p1, yo, p1) into one st, making 3 sts in the group

Ⅿ = make one st by picking up strand between last st worked and next st, and k into back of strand

𝕊 = slip decrease 5 sts together thus: sl 3 knitwise, one at a time, with yarn at back, drop yarn then *pass the 2nd st on right hand needle over the first (centre) st: sl the centre st back to left hand needle and pass the next st on left hand needle over it*; sl the centre st back to right hand needle and rep from * to * once more: p the centre st

⊟ⅬⅬⅬ = put the first st on cn and hold at back: k the next 2 sts, then p the st from cn

ⅬⅬⅬ⊟ = put the first 2 sts on cn and hold at front: p the next st, then k the 2 sts from cn

⊟⊟ⅬⅬⅬ = put the first 2 sts on cn and hold at back: k the next 2 sts, then p the 2 sts from cn

CHART B

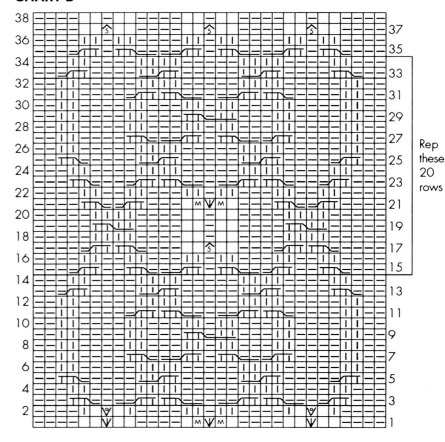

Rep these 20 rows

ⅬⅬⅬ⊟⊟ = put the first 2 sts on cn and hold at front: p the next 2 sts, then k the 2 sts from cn

⊟⊟ⅬⅬⅬ = put the first 2 sts on cn and hold at back: k the next 2 sts, then k the 2 sts from cn

ⅬⅬⅬⅬⅬ = put the first 2 sts on cn and hold at front: k the next 2 sts, then k the 2 sts from cn

ⅬⅬⅬ⊟ⅬⅬ = put the first 3 sts on cn and hold at front: k the next 2 sts, sl the p st back onto left hand needle and p it, then k the 2 sts from cn

---

All Sizes: Cast off 23[26,29] sts; place the next 41[43,45] sts on a holder; cast off the rem 23[26,29] sts.

FRONT

As back from ** to ***. Continue as set and work 94[94,114] rows of patts in total, ending after row 34 of chart B. Continue in main patt and chart A as set, and work row 35 through 38 of chart B over centre sts.

Second Size Only: Work a further 6 rows of main patt and chart A as set, and work reverse st.st. over the centre 19 sts.

All Sizes – Shape Neck
Keeping continuity as far as possible, patt 34[37,40]; place the next 19[21,23] sts on a holder; leave the rem sts on a spare

needle. Turn and shape left side as follows:-
* Cast off 2 sts at beg of next and foll alt row. Dec 1 st at neck edge of next 2 rows, then on every foll alt row 5 times. 23[26,29] sts rem. ** Continue straight in patt for a further 4 rows. Cast off all sts.

With right side facing, rejoin yarn to sts on spare needle and keeping continuity as far as possible, patt to end of row. Patt 1 more row, then shape neck as left side from * to **. Continue straight in patt for a further 3 rows. Cast off all sts.

SLEEVES

With 3¾mm (US5) needles and 2 strands of yarn A, cast on 42[46,46] sts. Join in 2 strands of yarn B and work check pattern as back for 8[10,10] rows. Break off both strands of yarn B.

Next Row – Increase
K3[3,2]; * m1, k5[8,6]; rep from * to the last 4[3,2] sts; m1, k4[3,2]. 50[52,54] sts.

Next Row: Change to 4½mm (US7) needles and p21[22,23]; k8; p21[22,23]. Beg at row 1 and set patts as follows:- Work main patt over the first 21[22,23] sts; chart A over the next 8 sts; main patt over the rem 21[22,23] sts.

First Size Only: Work row 3 of main patt, p1, * k2, p2; rep from *.
Third Size Only: Work row 3 of main patt, k1, p2, * k2, p2; rep from *.

All Sizes: Continue as set and increase 1 st at each side of 5th and every foll 5th[4th,4th] row until there are 84[92,100] sts. Work all increased sts into main patt. Continue straight in patts until

*Enjoying a fishing trip, 'Galway' (left), 'Iona'
(centre – page 81) and 'Cashel' (right – page
77) are ideal companions and protection
against the elements.*

sleeve measures 34.5[37,41]cm
13½[14½,16]in. Cast off all sts.

FINISHING

Do not press pieces. Join back and front at
left shoulder seam.

NECKBAND

With right side facing, 3¾mm (US5)
needles and 2 strands of yarn A, pick up
and k the 41[43,45] sts from back neck
holder; knit up 16 sts to front holder; pick
up and k the 19[21,23] sts from holder;
knit up 16 sts to cast off edge. 92[96,100]
sts. K1, p1 rib for 5[7,7] rows. Break off
yarn A. Change to 4½mm (US7) needles
and with 2 strands of yarn B, p right side
rows and k wrong side rows for 7[9,9]
rows. Cast off loosely and evenly,
knitwise.

Sew up right shoulder and neckband seam.
Place centre top of sleeves at shoulder
seams and sew on sleeves between
markers. Press seams lightly on wrong
side. Sew up side and sleeve seams, then
press seams lightly on wrong side.

A = 40 [44, 47]cm
B = 42.5 [46, 50]cm
C = 4 [5, 5]cm
D = 23.5 [25, 27]cm
E = 19 [21, 23]cm
F = 11 [12, 13]cm
G = 18 [20, 21]cm
H = 23 [24, 25]cm
I = 38 [42, 46]cm
J = 34.5 [37, 41]cm

A = 15¾ [17¼, 18½]in
B = 16¾ [18, 19¾]in
C = 1½ [2, 2]in
D = 9¼ [9¾, 10¾]in
E = 7½ [8¼, 9]in
F = 4¼ [4¾, 5¼]in
G = 7¼ [7¾, 8]in
H = 9 [9½, 9¾]in
I = 15 [16½, 18]in
J = 13½ [14½, 16]in

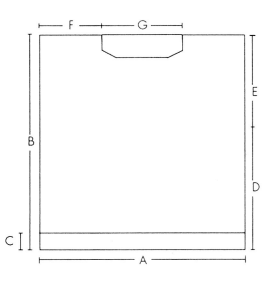

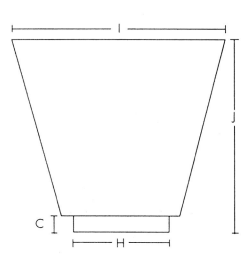

KILRONAN
SWEATER
IN CELTIC KNOTWORK

RATING

★ ★ ★

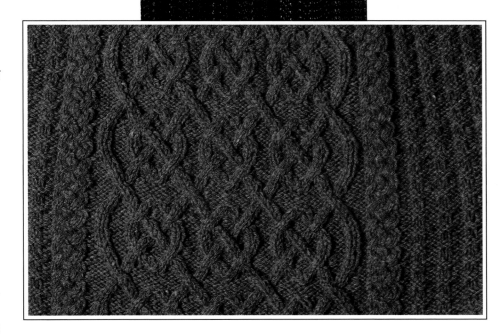

SIZES
To fit bust 86-91[97-102]cm 34-36[38-40]in.
Directions for the larger size are given in parenthesis. Where there is only one set of figures, it applies to both sizes.

KNITTED MEASUREMENTS
Underarm 104[110]cm 41[43½]in.
Length from top of shoulder 65[68]cm 25½[26½]in.
Sleeve length 42cm 16½in.

MATERIALS
Yarn: 14[15] 50g balls of Rowan Lambswool Tweed (184 – Bluster).

1 Pair each 3¾mm (US5) and 4mm (US6) needles. 1 Set of double-pointed or 40cm (16in) circular needles for collar. 1 Cable needle. 2 Stitch holders. 1 Darning needle.

TENSION (GAUGE)
13 sts and 17 rows to 5cm (2in), measured over main patt, using 4mm (US6) needles.
To work main patt, see STITCHES below.

STITCHES
Main Patt: Worked at each side of back, front and sleeves, as follows:- **Row 1**: (right side) Purl. **Row 2**: Knit. **Row 3**: P2, * k2, p2; rep from *. **Row 4**: K2, * p2, k2; rep from *. Rep these 4 rows. **Chart Patts**: Odd numbered rows are right side, and even numbered rows are wrong side. The cabled sts are worked in st.st. on a reverse st.st. background, as indicated on charts.
Note: The stitch number in the cabled panels in charts B and C increases at the beginning and decreases to the original number at the end of each panel. This is indicated on the charts.

This tunic-style sweater, with a shaped waist in single rib, is knitted in a heathery tweed yarn that reflects the colours of the Irish countryside. The knotwork design is embossed on a broad centre front panel.

I have based the shape of this sweater on traditional Scottish costumes, with a ribbed waist that can be worn belted and set-in sleeves for a slightly more squared shoulder line. The centre panel, composed of interlaced knotwork with ring knots, is a knitted version of an illustration from the book Celtic Knotwork by Iain Bain. I have used a narrower panel for the sleeves, and bordered all the panels with a plaited cable. It is important in this type of traditional knotwork that all the ringwork panels are closed so that there are no broken lines.

BACK
* With 4mm (US6) needles, cast on 131[139] sts. K 7[9] rows. **Next Row**: (wrong side) K38[42]; p8; k39; p8; k38[42]. Beg at row 1 of all patts, and set patts as follows:-
Work main patt over the first 38[42] sts; chart A over the next 8 sts; chart B over the next 39 sts, increasing as indicated; chart A over the next 8 sts; main patt over the rem 38[42] sts.

Continue as set, repeating the 4 rows of main patt and chart A, and work the first 34 rows of chart B once only, then repeat from row 15 through row 38 once. 58 patt rows in total.

Second Size Only: Work 2 more rows of main patt and chart A as set, and work reverse st.st. over the 39 centre panel sts.

Both Sizes – Decrease
K1[0], * k2tog, k3; rep from * 7[8] times in all; k2tog; k55; k2tog; * k3, k2tog; rep from * 7[8] times in all; k1[0].
115[121] sts.
Change to 3¾mm (US5) needles and k1, p1 rib for 9cm 3½in, with wrong side facing for next row.

CHART B

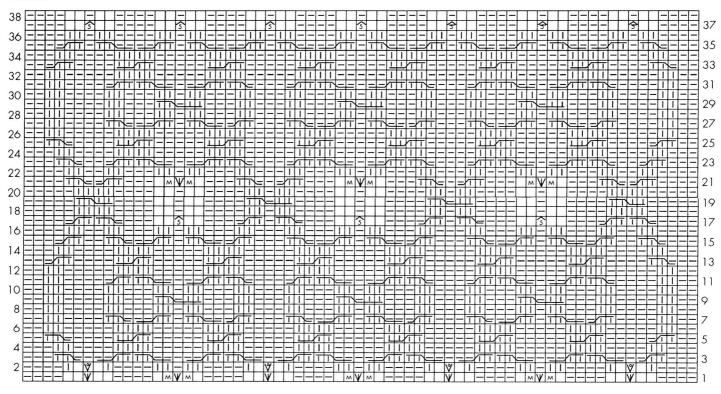

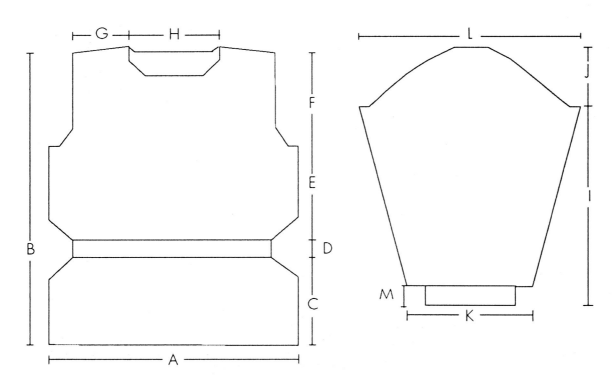

A = 52 [55]cm
B = 65 [68]cm
C = 20.5 [22]cm
D = 9cm
E = 15cm
F = 20.5 [22]cm
G = 10 [10.5]cm
H = 18 [19]cm
I = 42cm
J = 14 [15.5]cm
K = 27.5cm
L = 44.5 [46.5]cm
M = 7cm

A = 20½ [21¾]in
B = 25½ [26½]in
C = 8 [8½]in
D = 3½in
E = 6in
F = 8 [8½]in
G = 4 [4¼]in
H = 7 [7¼]in
I = 16½in
J = 5½ [6]in
K = 10¾in
L = 17½ [18¼]in
M = 2¾in

CHART A

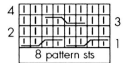

CHART C

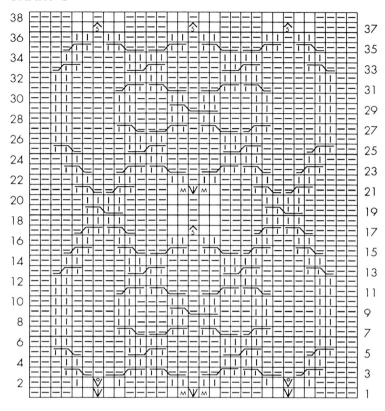

KEY

☐ = no stitch

Ⅱ = k on RS rows and p on WS rows

⊟ = p on RS rows and k on WS rows

Ⅴ = (k1b, k1) in one st, then insert left hand needle point behind the vertical strand that runs down between the 2 sts just made and k into this strand making the 3rd st of the group

Ⅴ = (p1, yo, p1) into one st, making 3 sts in the group

Ⅿ = make one st by picking up strand between last st worked and next st, and k into back of strand

⑤ = slip decrease 5 sts together thus: sl 3 knitwise, one at a time, with yarn

at back, drop yarn then *pass the 2nd st on right hand needle over the first (centre) st: sl the centre st back to left hand needle and pass the next st on left hand needle over it*; sl the centre st back to right hand needle and rep from * to * once more: p the centre st

⊟⁄Ⅲ = put the first st on cn and hold at back: k the next 2 sts, then p the st from cn

ⅢⅤ⊟ = put the first 2 sts on cn and hold at front: p the next st, then k the 2 sts from cn

⊟⁄ⅢⅢ = put the first 2 sts on cn and hold at back: k the next 2 sts, then p

the 2 sts from cn

ⅢⅤ⊟⊟ = put the first 2 sts on cn and hold at front: p the next 2 sts, then k the 2 sts from cn

ⅡⅡⅤⅢ = put the first 2 sts on cn and hold at back: k the next 2 sts, then k the 2 sts from cn

ⅢⅤⅡⅡ = put the first 2 sts on cn and hold at front: k the next 2 sts, then k the 2 sts from cn

ⅢⅤⅢⅢ = put the first 3 sts on cn and hold at front: k the next 2 sts, sl the p st back onto left hand needle and p it, then k the 2 sts from cn

---

Next Row – Increase
K2[1], * m1, k4; rep from * 7[8] times in all; m1; p8; k39; p8; m1; * k4, m1; rep from * 7[8] times in all; k2[1]. 131[139] sts. Change to 4mm (US6) needles.

Second Size Only: Work main patt over the first 42 sts; chart A over the next 8 sts; reverse st.st. over the next 39 sts; chart A over the next 8 sts; main patt over the rem 42 sts. Work 1 more row as set.

Both Sizes: Beg at row 1[3] of main patt and chart A and at row 1 of chart B, work main patt over the first 38[42] sts; chart A over the next 8 sts; chart B over the next

39 sts, increasing as indicated; chart A over the next 8 sts; main patt over the rem 38 [42] sts.

Continue as set and work the first 34 rows of chart B once only, and thereafter rep from row 15 through row 34. Continue until piece measures 15cm 6in from end of rib, with right side facing for next row.

Shape Armholes
Keeping continuity of patt, cast off 6[7] sts at beg of next 2 rows. Cast off 2 sts at beg of next 4 rows. Dec 1 st at each side of next and foll alt rows until 21[23] main

patt sts rem at each side. ** Continue straight as set until 102 rows of chart B have been worked in total. Then continue in main patt and chart A as set and work row 23 through row 38 of chart B.

Second Size Only: Work 2 more rows in main patt and chart A as set, and work the 39 centre sts in reverse st.st.

Both Sizes – Shape Shoulder and Back Neck
Keeping continuity of patt, cast off 9 sts; patt 20[21] sts; place the next 39[41] sts

Early morning mists can be deceptively cool. Keep warm after a gallop in 'Kilronan' with its long lines and snug-fitting polo collar worked in an elegant twisted rib.

on a holder. Turn and work right shoulder as follows:-
Row 1: P2tog, patt to end. **Row 2**: Cast off 9 sts, patt to end. **Row 3**: P2tog, patt to end. Cast off the rem 9[10] sts.

With right side facing, rejoin yarn to the rem sts, and keeping continuity, patt as set to end of row. **Next row**: Cast off 9 sts, patt to end. Complete as right shoulder, reversing all shapings.

FRONT
As back from * to **. Continue as set until 82 rows of chart B have beeen worked in total. Continue in main patt and chart A as set, and work row 23 through row 38 of chart B.

Second Size Only: Work 2 more rows in main patt and chart A as set, and work 39 centre sts in reverse st.st.

Both Sizes – Shape Front Neck
Keeping continuity of patt, and working reverse st.st. over centre panel sts, patt 39[40] sts; place the next 19[21] sts on a holder; leave the rem sts on a spare needle. Turn and work left neck and shoulder as follows:-
* Keeping continuity of patts as far as possible, dec 1 st at neck edge of next 4 rows. Then dec 1 st at neck edge of foll 8 alt rows. AT THE SAME TIME, when front corresponds in length with back at shoulder, with right side facing for next row, shape shoulder by casting off 9 sts at beg of next and foll alt row. Then cast off the rem 9[10] sts on next alt row. **

With right side facing, rejoin yarn to the rem sts of front, and working rem centre panel sts in reverse st.st. and keeping continuity of chart A and main patt, patt to end of row. Complete as left neck and shoulder from * to **, reading 'wrong side facing' at shoulder shaping.

SLEEVES
With 3¼mm (US5) needles, cast on 54 sts. Work cable rib as follows:-
Row 1: (wrong side) * K2, p2; rep from * to the last 2 sts; k2. **Row 2**: * P2, RT (Right Twist) thus – k2tog and leave the sts on the left needle, then k into the first of the 2 sts again and slip both sts to right

needle; rep from * to the last 2 sts; p2.
Row 3: As row 1. **Row 4**: * P2, k2; rep to the last 2 sts; p2. Rep these 4 rows until cuff measures 7cm 2¾in, with right side facing for next row.

Next Row – Increase
Rib 3, * m1, rib 3; rep from * to end of row. 71 sts.
Change to 4mm (US6) needles. **Next Row**: P18; k8; p19; k8; p18. Beg at row 1 of patts and set patts as follows:-
Work main patt over the first 18 sts; chart A over the next 8 sts; chart C over the next 19 sts, increasing as indicated, and working rows 1 through 34 once only, and thereafter rep rows 15 through 34; chart A over the next 8 sts; main patt over the rem 18 sts. Continue as set and increase 1 st at each end of 3rd[next] and every foll 5th row, working all increased sts into main patt, until there are 115[119] sts. Continue straight as set until 118 rows of patt have been worked in total.

Shape Cap
Keeping continuity of patt, cast off 6[7] sts at beg of next 2 rows. Cast off 2 sts at beg of next 4 rows. Dec 1 st at each end of next and foll 0[3] alt rows. Dec 1 st at each end of every foll row until 13[15] sts rem.

AT THE SAME TIME, when 142 rows of chart C have been worked from beg, work rows 23 through 38 of chart. Thereafter, work the rem centre panel sts in reverse st.st. Cast off the rem 13[15] sts.

FINISHING
Do not press pieces. Join back and front at shoulders. Press seams lightly on wrong side.

COLLAR
With double-pointed or circular 3¼mm (US5) needles and right side of work facing, pick up and p the 39[41] sts from back neck holder; purl up 27 sts to front neck holder; pick up and p the 19[21] sts from holder; purl up 27 sts to complete round. 112[116] sts. Place a marker at beg of rnd and work cable rib as follows:-
Rnd 1: * k2, p2; rep to end of rnd. **Rnd 2**: * RT, p2; rep from * to end of rnd. **Rnds 3 and 4**: As rnd 1. Rep these 4 rounds until collar measures 15cm 6in. Cast off all sts loosely and evenly in rib.
Sew up side and sleeve seams. Press seams lightly on wrong side, omitting all ribs. Place centre top of sleeve cap at shoulder seam and sew in sleeve, easing cap around armhole.

CELTIC
SPIRALS

TUROE
CELTIC SPIRAL SWEATER

RATING
★ ★ ★

SIZES
To fit bust 81-86[91-97,102-107]cm 32-34[36-38,40-42]in.
Directions for larger sizes are given in parenthesis. Where there is only one set of figures, it applies to all sizes.

KNITTED MEASUREMENTS
Underarm 110[115,120]cm 43[45½,47]in.
Length from top of shoulder 63[66.5,69.5]cm 24¾[26,26¾]in.
Sleeve length 41[43,46]cm 16¼[17,18]in.

MATERIALS
Yarn: Rowan Silk/Wool; Silkstones; Wool/Cotton; Donegal Tweed.

A. Camel Silk/Wool (851) 180[200,200]g; **B.** Ecru Silk/Wool (857) 100g; **C.** Coral Silk/Wool (855) 60g; **D.** Donkey Silk/Wool (856) 60[80,80]g; **E.** Moss Green Silk/Wool (852) 100g; **F.** Marble Silkstones (833) 50g; **G.** Blue Mist Silkstones (832) 25[50,50]g; **H.** Dried Rose Silkstones (825) 25[50,50]g; **I.** Mayfly Silkstones (821) 25g; **J.** Dragonfly Silkstones (823) 50g; **K.** Alabaster Wool/Cotton (909) 200[240,240]g; **L.** Kashmir Wool/Cotton (910) 80[120,120]g; **M.** Dove Wool/Cotton (911) 80g; **N.** Oatmeal Donegal Tweed (469) 25[50,50]g.

1 Pair each 4mm (US6) needles. 1 Set of double-pointed or 40cm (16in) circular 4mm (US6) needles for neckband. 2 Stitch holders. Stitch markers. 1 Darner.

TENSION (GAUGE)
22 sts and 28 rows to 10cm (4in), measured over chart A patt, using 4mm (US6) needles.

The magical mood of mountains and moorlands is captured in this stunning sweater with its bold swirling shapes in subtle colours and textures. This is a challenging design for a competent knitter, but the result is rewarding.

STITCHES
Chart A patt: Worked entirely in st.st. Odd numbered rows are right side, even numbered rows are wrong side. Use separate lengths of yarn for each area of colour. Link one colour to the next by twisting them around each other where they meet on the wrong side to avoid gaps. See page 137 for intarsia knitting. The yarns are used in combination throughout e.g. AK means use 1 strand of A and 1 strand of K; CC means use two strands of C. **Chart B patt**: All rounds are worked in k. Each rnd begins on right side of chart, as indicated. The yarn not in immediate use is stranded across the wrong side. The yarns are used in combination throughout, as in chart A.

BACK
* With 4mm (US6) needles and AK, cast on 119[125,129] sts. Work st.st. for 2.5cm 1in, with wrong side facing for next row. K 1 row (hemline). Joining in and breaking off colours as required, work patt from chart A until back measures 37.5[40.5,42]cm 14¾[15¾,16¼]in from hemline. ** Place a marker at each end of row and continue working chart patt through row 168[176,182].

Shape Neck
Keeping continuity of chart, patt 38[40,41]; place the next 43[45,47] sts on a holder; leave the rem sts on a spare needle. Turn, and keeping continuity of chart, dec 1 st at neck edge of next 2 rows. Patt 1 row straight, then dec 1 st at neck edge of next row. 35[37,38] sts rem. Patt 1 row straight. Cast off evenly.

With right side facing, and keeping continuity of chart, k38[40,41] from spare needle. Then complete as previous side, reversing shaping and working 2 rows straight before casting off, as indicated on chart.

FRONT
As back from * to **. Place a marker at each end of row and continue working chart patt through row 160[166,172].

Shape Neck
Keeping continuity of chart, patt 44[47,48]; place the next 31[31,33] sts on

The source for this dramatic design is the granite pillar at Turoe, County Galway that is carved with abstract Celtic spirals. To convey the grainy, glinting surface of the granite I have used a mixture of shiny and dull silk and wool yarns in the appropriate colours. The regular pattern on the neckline of this sweater echoes the rhythm of the steps around the base of the stone.

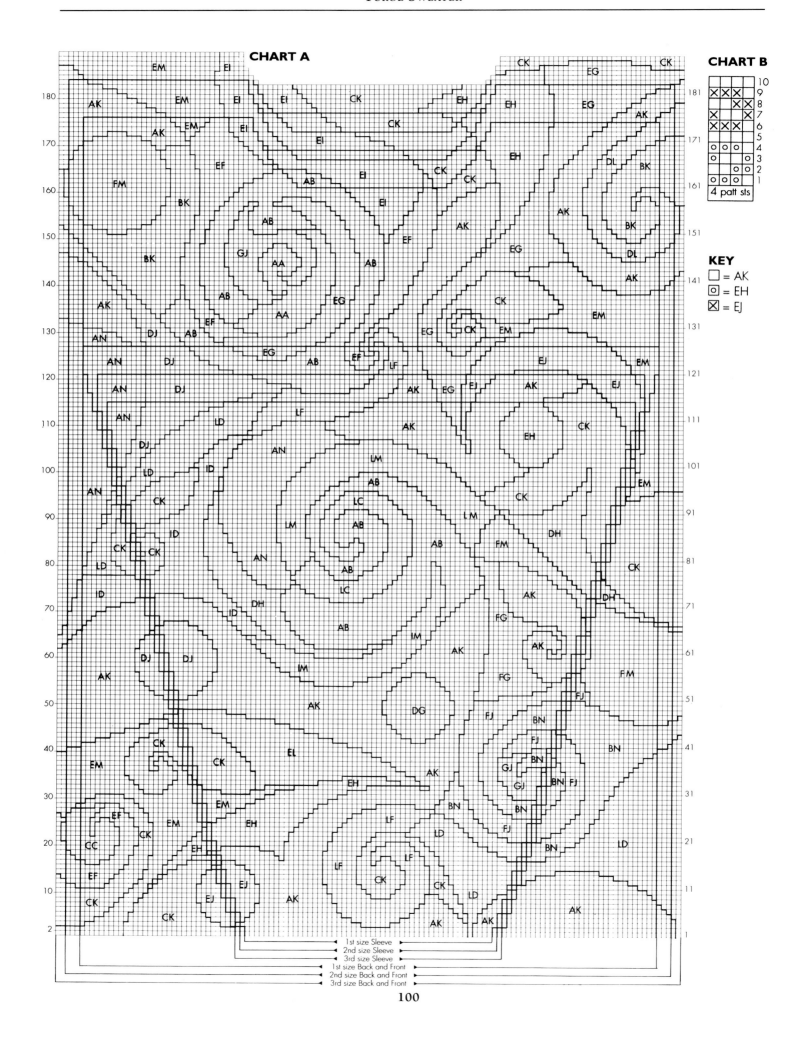

CHART A

CHART B

10
9
8
7
6
5
4
3
2
1
4 patt sts

KEY
□ = AK
⊙ = EH
⊠ = EJ

◄ 1st size Sleeve ►
◄ 2nd size Sleeve ►
◄ 3rd size Sleeve ►
◄ 1st size Back and Front ►
◄ 2nd size Back and Front ►
◄ 3rd size Back and Front ►

a holder; leave the rem sts on a spare needle. Turn, and keeping continuity of chart, dec 1 st at neck edge of next 6 rows. Patt 1 row straight, then dec 1 st at neck edge of next and every foll alt row 3[4,4] times in all. 35[37,38] sts rem. Patt 1 row straight. Cast off evenly.

With right side facing, and keeping continuity of chart, patt 44[47,48] from spare needle and complete as previous side, reversing shaping and working 2 rows straight before casting off, as indicated on chart.

SLEEVES
With 4mm (US6) needles and AK, cast on 51[53,55] sts. Work st.st. for 2.5cm 1in, with wrong side facing for next row. K 1

row (hemline). Then joining in and breaking off colours as required, work patt from Chart A as indicated, increasing 1 st at each end of every 3rd row 7 times. 65[67,69] sts. Then continue to increase on every foll 4th row until there are 109[113,119] sts. Continue straight in patt through row 114[120,126] of chart. Cast off evenly.

FINISHING
Darn in loose ends. Press pieces lightly on wrong side. Join back and front at shoulder seams. Place centre top of sleeves at shoulder seams and sew sleeves to body between markers. Press seams lightly on wrong side. Sew up side and sleeve seams and press seams lightly on wrong side.

Turn body and sleeve hems to wrong side at hemline and slip stitch in position.

NECKBAND
With double-pointed or circular 4mm (US6) needles and AK, pick up and k the 43[45,47] sts from back neck holder; knit up 19[20,20] sts to front holder; pick up and k the 31[31,33] sts from holder; knit up 19[20,20] sts to complete round. 112[116,120] sts.

Joining in and breaking off colours as required, work the 10 rnds of patt from chart B, repeating the 4 patt sts 28[29,30] times in the rnd. With AK, p 1 rnd (hemline), then k 10 rnds. Cast off loosely. Turn neckband to inside at hemline and stitch in place. Press hems lightly.

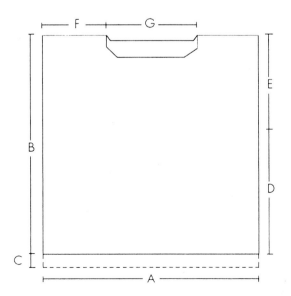

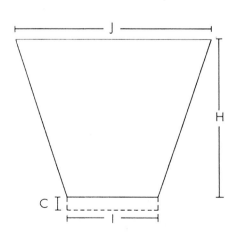

A = 55 [57.5, 60]cm
B = 63 [66.5, 69.5]cm
C = 2.5cm
D = 37.5 [40.5, 42]cm
E = 25.5 [26, 27.5]cm
F = 16.5 [17, 18]cm
G = 22 [23.5, 24]cm
H = 41 [43, 46]cm
I = 23.5 [24, 25.5]cm
J = 51 [52, 55]cm

A = 21½ [22¾, 23½]in
B = 24¾ [26, 26¾]in
C = 1in
D = 14¾ [15¾, 16¼]in
E = 10 [10¼, 10¾]in
F = 6½ [6¾, 7]in
G = 8½ [9¼, 9½]in
H = 16¼ [17, 18]in
I = 9¼ [9½, 10]in
J = 20 [20½, 21½]in

ROINEVAL
CELTIC SPIRAL SWEATER

RATING

★ ★ ★ ★

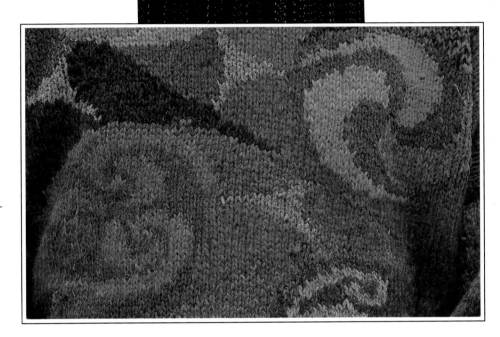

SIZES
One size fits chest/bust 86-112cm 34-42in.

KNITTED MEASUREMENTS
Underarm 136cm 53½in.
Length from top of shoulder 67.5cm 26½in.
Sleeve length 44.5cm 17½in.

MATERIALS
Yarn: Rowan Donegal Tweed; Fine Cotton Chenille; Silkstones; Kid/Silk; DDK; Lambswool Tweed; LDK.

A. Rainforest Donegal Tweed (489) 75g;
B. Elderberry Donegal Tweed (490) 50g;
C. Bay Donegal Tweed (485) 50g;
D. Juniper Donegal Tweed (482) 50g;
E. Roseberry Donegal Tweed (480) 50g;
F. Leaf Donegal Tweed (481) 25g;
G. Privet Fine Chenille (394) 75g; **H.** Plum Fine Chenille (386) 50g; **I.** Lacquer Fine Chenille (388) 75g; **J.** Willow Fine Chenille (395) 25g; **K.** Mole Fine Chenille (380) 25g; **L.** Turquoise Fine Chenille (383) 25g; **M.** Cyclamen Fine Chenille (385) 25g; **N.** Teal Silkstones (828) 75g; **O.** Beetle Silkstones (834) 75g; **P.** Dried Rose Silkstones (825) 50g; **Q.** Chilli Silkstones (826) 50g; **R.** Garnet Kid/Silk (992) 100g; **S.** Holly Kid/Silk (990) 50g; **T.** Steel Blue Kid/Silk (991) 125g; **U.** Old Gold Kid/Silk (989) 25g; **V.** Crushed Berry Kid/Silk (993) 25g; **W.** Ruby Red DDK (651) 50g; **X.** Rose Pink DDK (70) 50g; **Y.** Russet DDK (663) 50g; **Z.** Bluster Lambswool Tweed (184) 50g.

1 Pair each 4mm (US6) and 5mm (US8) needles. 1 Set of double-pointed or 40cm (16in) circular 4mm (US6) needles for neckband. 2 Stitch holders. Stitch markers. Darning needle.

TENSION (GAUGE)
18 sts and 24 rows to 10cm (4in), measured over chart patt, using 5mm (US8) needles.

'Roineval' is a masterpiece of intarsia knitting. The richly-patterned stocking stitch fabric uses 26 colours to represent the sky, sunrises, sunsets, water and moorlands of a native Celtic landscape.

I find a strong connection between the abstract Celtic spirals and the hill which occupies a central and dominant position in the view from my home on the Isle of Lewis. Roineval rises in an elegant sweeping curve from the west. Throughout the day an ever-changing play of light and shade on the landscape of hill, moorland and loch makes a fascinating study of shape and colour that I have translated into this design. This fabulous one-size sweater, knitted in a variety of different textured yarns, will fit a range of sizes comfortably.

STITCHES
2/2 rib: K2 in first colour, p2 in second colour, stranding the yarns evenly across wrong side. **Chart patt**: Worked entirely in st.st. Odd numbered rows are right side, even numbered rows are wrong side. Use separate lengths of yarn for each area of colour. Link one colour to the next by twisting them around each other where they meet on the wrong side to avoid gaps. See page 137 for intarsia knitting. The yarns are used in combination throughout e.g. CG means use 1 strand of C and 1 strand of G; EE means use 2 strands of E.

BACK
* With 4mm (US6) needles and 1 strand of A combined with 1 strand of T, cast on 108 sts.
Joining in and breaking off colours as required, work 2/2 rib as follows:-
Row 1: K2 AT, p2 EI. **Row 2**: K2 EI, p2 AT. **Row 3**: K2 AT, p2 EM. **Row 4**: K2 EM, p2 AT. **Row 5**: K2 BN, p2 EK. **Row 6**: K2 EK, p2 BN. **Row 7**: K2 BN, p2 KY. **Row 8**: K2 KY, p2 BN. **Row 9**: K2 CO, p2 RP. **Row 10**: K2 RP, p2 CO. Rep rows 1 – 10 until rib measures 6cm 2½in, with wrong side facing for next row.

Knitted throughout with two strands of yarn, varying the colours and textures for maximum effect, this sweater is extra thick to keep out the coldest weather. Worn here by a man, it is also perfect for a woman who prefers the generous sizing.

Next Row – Increase
With colours as for next row of rib – rib 1; m1; rib 8; * m1, rib 9; rep from * to the last 9 sts; m1; rib 8; m1; rib 1. 121 sts. Change to 5mm (US8) needles and, joining in and breaking off colours as required, work the patt from chart until back measures 40.5cm 16in from cast on edge. ** Place a marker at each end of row and continue working chart patt through row 144. Cast off 43 sts; place the centre 35 sts on a holder; cast off the rem 43 sts.

FRONT
As back from * to **. Mark each end of row. Continue working chart through row 124.

Shape Neck
Patt 55; place the next 11 sts on a holder; leave the rem sts on a spare needle. Turn and work left neck/shoulder as follows:- *** Keeping continuity of chart patt, cast off 3 sts, patt to end of row. Dec 1 st at neck edge of next 3 rows, then on every foll alt row 6 times. 43 sts rem. Continue straight through row 144 of chart. Cast off all sts. ****

With right side facing and keeping continuity of chart, patt the sts from spare needle. Patt the next wrong side row, then complete right neck/shoulder as left, from *** to ****.

SLEEVES
With 4mm (US6) needles and 1 strand of A combined with 1 strand of T, cast on 40 sts. Joining in and breaking off colours as required, work 2/2 rib in colours as back for 6cm 2½in, ending with wrong side facing for next row.
Next Row – Increase
With colours as for next row of rib – rib 1; m1; rib 3; * m1, rib 4; rep from * to the last 4 sts; m1; rib 3; m1; rib 1. 51 sts.

Change to 5mm (US8) needles and, joining in and breaking off colours as required, work the patt from chart, increasing 1 st at each end of every 4th row, as indicated, until there are 95 sts. Continue straight through row 90 of chart. Cast off all sts.

FINISHING
Darn in loose ends. Press pieces lightly on wrong side, omitting ribs. Join back and front at shoulder seams. Place centre top of sleeves at shoulder seams and sew sleeves to body between markers. Press seams lightly on wrong side. Sew up side and sleeve seams, then press lightly on wrong side, omitting ribs.

NECKBAND
With right side facing, set of double-pointed or circular 4mm (US6) needles, and 1 strand of C combined with 1 strand of O, pick up and k the 35 sts from back neck holder; knit up 19 sts to front neck holder; pick up and k the 11 sts from holder; knit up 19 sts to complete round. 84 sts. Joining in and breaking off colours as required, work 2/2 rib as follows:-
Rnds 1 and 2: K2 CO, p2 RP. **Rnds 3 and 4**: K2 BN, p2 KY. **Rnds 5 and 6**: K2 BN, p2 EK. **Rnds 7 and 8**: K2 AT, p2 EM.

With AT, cast off loosely and evenly, purlwise. Darn in all loose ends.

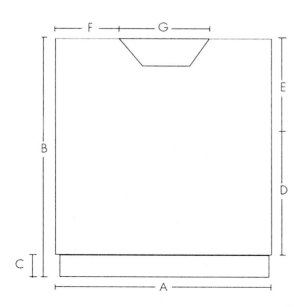

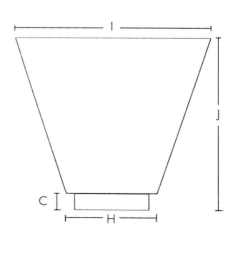

A = 68cm	26¾in
B = 67.5cm	26½in
C = 6cm	2½in
D = 40.5cm	16in
E = 27cm	10½in
F = 24cm	9½in
G = 20cm	7¾in
H = 29cm	11¼in
I = 54cm	21in
J = 44.5cm	17½in

DONEGAL
CELTIC SPIRAL
SWEATER

RATING
★ ★ ★

SIZES
To fit chest/bust 86-91 [97-102,107-112]cm
34-36 [38-40,42-44]in.
Directions for larger sizes are given in
parenthesis. Where there is only one set of
figures, it applies to all sizes.

KNITTED MEASUREMENTS
Underarm 104 [114,123]cm
41 [44¾,48½]in.
Length from top of shoulder 63[65,67]cm
24¾[25½,26¼]in.
Sleeve seam 45[47,49]cm
17¾[18½,19¼]in.

MATERIALS
Yarn: Rowan Donegal Tweed.

A. Rainforest (489) 50g; **B.** Roseberry
(480) 50g; **C.** Bay (485) 75g; **D.** Bark
(475) 75[100,100]g; **E.** Sapphire (486)
50[50,75]g; **F.** Tarragon (477) 50[75,75]g;
G. Elderberry (490) 50[50,75]g;
H. Bramble (484) 50[75,75]g; **I.** Juniper
(482) 50[75,75]g; **J.** Pickle (483) 25[50,50]g;
K. Shale (467) 25g.

---

1 Set of double-pointed or circular 2¾mm
(US2) and 3¼mm (US3) needles. 2 Stitch
holders. 2 Safety pins. Stitch markers.
Darning needle.

TENSION (GAUGE)
15 sts and 15 rows to 5cm (2in), measured
over pattern, using 3¼mm (US3) needles,
and working the patt on right side only,
breaking off the yarns at the end of every
row.
See page 137 for further details of making
a Fair Isle swatch.

STITCHES
2/2 rib: K2 with first colour, p2 with
second colour, stranding the yarns evenly
across wrong side. **Chart patt:** K
every round, and on two-colour rounds,
strand the yarn not in immediate use
evenly across wrong side. On stretches of
more than 7 sts in one colour, weave in
yarn not in use at centre of stretch. **Steeks:**
Worked at armholes, and neck, and later
cut up centre to form openings. The steek
is worked over 10 sts. K these sts on every

round, and on two-colour rounds, k each
st and round in alt colours. Do not weave
in newly joined in or broken off yarns at
centre of first steek. Instead leave approx.
5cm (2in) tail when joining in and
breaking off yarns. **Edge stitch:** Worked at
each side of armhole steeks and k in
background colours on every round. Sts
for sleeves are knitted up from edge
stitches. **Cross stitch:** With darning
needle, overcast raw edge of steek to
strands on wrong side of knitting, and
after sewing to end, reverse the direction
to form cross stitches. See page 137 for
full illustrations of steeks, edge stitches
and cross stitch.

BODY
With 2¾mm (US2) needles and A, cast on
284[308,332] sts. Mark the first st of rnd,
and making sure that cast on edge is not
twisted, work 2/2 rib as follows:-
Rnd 1: K2 A, p2 B. **Rnd 2:** K2 C, p2 B.
Rnd 3: K2 C, p2 D. **Rnds 4 & 5:** K2 E, p2
D. **Rnd 6:** K2 E, p2 F. **Rnds 7 & 8:** K2 G,
p2 F. **Rnd 9:** K2 H, p2 F. **Rnds 10 & 11:**
K2 H, p2 I. **Rnd 12:** K2 J, p2 I. **Rnd 13:**
K2 J, p2 K. **Rnds 14 through 25:**
Working back, as rnds 12 through 1.

Next rnd – Increase
First size: With A, m1, k11; (m1, k12) 10
times; (m1, k11) twice; (m1, k12) 10

Here I wanted to create a regular spiral pattern similar to those that are a common feature on stonework, metalwork and manuscripts. This particular design works very well for a sweater in the traditional Fair Isle style where the motif is repeated against a background of bands of different colours. Rustic shades of a Donegal tweed yarn have been used throughout.

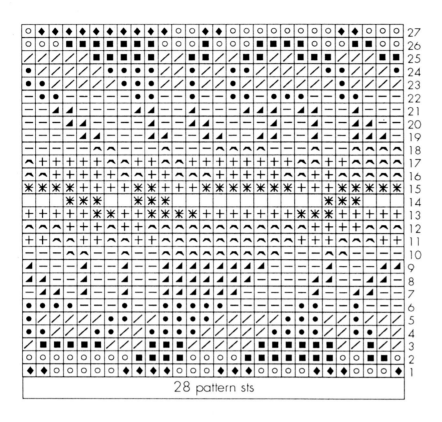

KEY

◆	= A
○	= B
■	= C
╱	= D
●	= E
⊟	= F
◢	= G
⌃	= H
⊞	= I
✳	= J
☐	= K

28 pattern sts

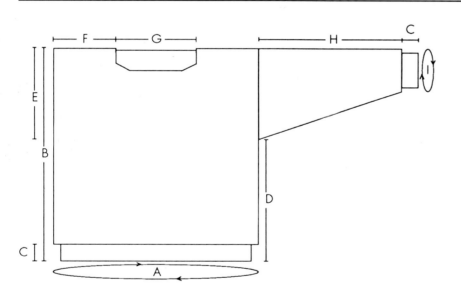

A = 104 [114, 123]cm   41 [44³⁄₄, 48¹⁄₂]in
B = 63 [65, 67]cm   23³⁄₄ [25¹⁄₂, 26¹⁄₄]in
C = 7cm   2³⁄₄in ·
D = 39 [39.5, 40]cm   15¹⁄₄ [15¹⁄₂, 15³⁄₄]in
E = 24 [25.5, 27]cm   9¹⁄₂ [10, 10¹⁄₂]in
F = 16.5 [18.5, 20.5]cm   6¹⁄₂ [7¹⁄₄, 8]in
G = 19 [19.5, 20]cm   7¹⁄₂ [7³⁄₄, 8]in
H = 38 [40, 42]cm   15 [15³⁄₄, 16¹⁄₂]in
I = 24 [25.5, 27]cm   9¹⁄₂ [10, 10¹⁄₂]in

times; m1, k11. 308 sts.
Second size: With A, (m1, k11) rep to end of rnd. 336 sts.
Third size: With A, (m1, k10) 5 times; (m1, k11) 6 times; (m1, k10) 10 times; (m1 k11) 6 times; (m1, k10) 5 times. 364 sts.
All sizes: Mark first st of rnd, change to 3¹⁄₄mm (US3) needles, and joining in and breaking off colours as required, work patt from chart, repeating the 28 patt sts 11[12,13] times in the rnd. Repeat the 27 patt rnds until body measures 39[39.5,40]cm 15¹⁄₄[15¹⁄₂,15³⁄₄]in from beg.

Next rnd – Work Armhole Steeks and Edge Sts
Place the first st of rnd on a safety pin. With colours as for next rnd of chart, cast on 6 sts, with alt colours; mark the first st cast on for beg of rnd and centre of first steek (the first 5 sts cast on are steek sts, the last st cast on is an edge st); keeping continuity of chart, patt over the next 153[167,181] sts of front; place the next st on a safety pin; with alt colours, cast on 12 sts (the first and last sts cast on are edge sts, the centre 10 sts are steek sts); keeping continuity of chart, patt over the 153[167,181] sts of back; with alt colours, cast on 6 sts (first st cast on is an edge st, the last 5 sts are steek sts). Work the steek sts in alt colours and the edge sts in darker colours throughout, and keeping continuity, work chart patt on front and back sts until piece measures 17[18,19]cm 6³⁄₄[7,7¹⁄₂]in from safety pin rnd.

Next Rnd – Begin Front Neck Shaping
With colours as for next rnd of chart, work 5 steek sts; k1 edge st; keeping continuity of chart, patt the next 59[65,71] sts of front; place the next 35[37,39] sts on a holder for front neck; with alt colours, cast on 10 steek sts; keeping continuity, work as set to end of rnd. Work front neck steek in alt colours, and keeping continuity, dec 1 st at each side of front neck steek on next 5 rnds. Work 1 rnd straight, then dec at each side of neck steek on next and

This delightful sweater, with a regular pattern of elegant scrolls, is knitted in toning shades of tweed yarn.

The magical blend of harmonizing colours continues into the ribbed edgings which are striped vertically as well as horizontally.

every foll alt rnd until 48[54,60] chart patt sts rem on each front shoulder. AT THE SAME TIME, when back measures 21.5[23,24.5] cm 8½[9,9½]in from safety pin rnd, shape back neck as follows:-
Continue as set to beg of 153[167,181] sts of back; patt the next 51[57,63] sts; place the next 51[53,55] sts on a holder for back neck; with alt colours, cast on 10 steek sts; keeping continuity, work as set to end of the rnd.

Continue as set, working straight at front neck edges when 48 [54,60] chart patt sts rem on front shoulders, and dec 1 st at each side of back neck steek on next and foll alt rnds until 48 [54,60] chart patt sts rem on back shoulders.
Next Rnd: Keeping continuity, patt 1 rnd straight, casting off all steek sts in the course of the rnd. With darker colour as for next rnd of chart, graft front and back shoulder and edge sts together. See page 137 for grafting. With A, sew backstitch up centre of first and last armhole steek sts. Cut open armhole steeks up centre, between 5th and 6th sts.

SLEEVES
With 3¼mm (US3) needles and A, pick up and k the st from safety pin, and mark this st for beg of rnd; knit up 141[149,157] sts evenly around armhole, working into loop of edge st next to chart patt. Patt sleeve as follows:-
With colours as for rnd 1 of chart , k marked st in A; patt the last 0[4,8] sts of chart; rep the 28 patt sts 5 times; patt the first 1[5,9] sts of chart.
Continue in chart patt as set, and work the marked st in darker colours throughout. Keeping continuity of patt, dec 1 st at each side of marked st on every 4th rnd until 132[140,148] sts rem. Then continue to dec as set on every foll 3rd rnd until 72[76,80] sts rem. Continue straight in patt until sleeve measures 38[40,42]cm 15[15¾, 16½] in. Change to 2¾mm (US2) needles, and with A dec for cuff as follows:-

First size: (K2tog, k7) rep to end of rnd. 64 sts.
Second size: (K2tog, k8) twice; (k2tog, k7) 4 times; (k2tog, k8) twice. 68 sts.

Third size: (K2tog, k8) rep to end of rnd. 72 sts.
All sizes: Work 25 rnds of 2/2 rib as body. With A, cast off all sts knitwise.

NECKBAND
With A, sew backstitch up centre of first and last front and back neck steek sts. Cut both steeks open up centre, between 5th and 6th sts. With 2¾mm (US2) needles and H, pick up and k the 51 [53,55] sts from back neck holder; knit up 27[29,31] sts evenly to front neck holder, working into shoulder st next to steek; pick up and k the 35[37,39] sts from holder; knit up 27[29,31] sts as previous, to complete rnd. 140[148,156] sts. Work 2/2 rib as follows:-

Rnd 1: K2 H, p2 F. **Rnds 2 & 3**: K2 G, p2 F. **Rnd 4**: K2 E, p2 F. **Rnds 5 & 6**: K2 E, p2 D. **Rnd 7**: K2 C, p2 D. **Rnd 8**: K2 C, p2 B. **Rnd 9**: K2 A, p2 B. With A, cast off all sts knitwise.

FINISHING
Trim all steeks to 3 sts and cross st in position. Darn in all loose ends. Press lightly on wrong side, omitting all ribs.

ARMAGH
CELTIC SPIRAL SWEATER

RATING

In this striking black and white sweater I have related two aspects of Celtic art from the earliest examples of metalwork and stonework. I like the contrast between the curving spirals used for the border and the straight lines of the fretwork pattern in the main fabric. I chose the dramatic monochrome colour scheme to accentuate the graphic quality of the design.

SIZES

To fit chest/bust 86-97[102-112]cm 34-38[40-44]in.
Directions for larger size are given in parenthesis. Where there is only one set of figures, it applies to both sizes.

KNITTED MEASUREMENTS

Underarm 114[130]cm 45[51¼]in.
Length from top of shoulder 67[69.5]cm 26½[27]in.
Sleeve length 47[50.5]cm 18½[20]in.

MATERIALS

Yarn: Rowan DDK.

A. Black (62) 450g; **B.** Off-white (649) 350[400]g.

1 Set of 4 double-pointed or circular 3¼mm (US3) and 3¾mm (US5) needles. 2 Stitch holders. 2 Safety pins. Stitch markers. Darning needle.

TENSION (GAUGE)

25 sts and 28 rows to 10cm (4in), measured over patt, using 3¾mm (US5) needles, and working the patt on the right side only, breaking off yarns at the end of every row. See page 137 for making a Fair Isle swatch.

STITCHES

2/2 rib: K2 with the first colour, p2 with second colour, stranding the yarns evenly across wrong side. **Chart patt**: K every rnd, and on two-colour rnds, strand the yarn not in immediate use evenly across wrong side. On stretches of more than 5 sts in one colour, weave in the yarn once at centre of stretch. **Steeks**: Worked at armholes and front neck, and later cut up centre to form openings. The steek is worked over 10 sts. K these sts on every rnd, and on two-colour rnds, k each st and rnd in alt colours. Do not weave in newly joined in or broken off yarns at the centre of first armhole steek. Instead leave approx. 5cm 2in tail when joining in and breaking off yarns. **Edge stitch**: Worked at each side of armhole steeks and k in background colour on every rnd. Sts for sleeves are knitted up from edge sts. **Cross stitch**: With darning needle, overcast raw edge of steeks to strands on

wrong side of knitting, and after sewing to end, reverse to form cross sts. See page 137 for full illustrations of steeks, edge stitches, and cross stitch.

BODY

With 3¼mm (US3) needles and yarn A, cast on 280[320] sts. Mark the first st of rnd, and making sure the cast on edge is not twisted, join in yarn B and work k2 A, p2 B rib for 5cm 2in.
Change to 3¾mm (US5) needles and work the 33 rnds of patt from chart A, repeating the 40 patt sts 7[8] times in the rnd. Then work the patt from chart B, repeating the 20 patt sts 14[16] times in the rnd. Rep the 20 patt rnds of chart B throughout, and continue until body measures 40[41]cm 15¾[16¼]in from beg. Break off yarns.

Work Armhole Steeks and Edge sts

Place the first st of rnd on a safety pin; with alt colours, cast on 6 sts (the first 5 sts cast on are steek sts, the last one is an edge st); mark the first st cast on for beg of rnd; keeping continuity of patt, patt the next 139[159] sts; place the next st on a safety pin ; with alt colours, cast on 12 sts (the first st and last one cast on are edge sts, the centre 10 are steek sts); keeping continuity of patt, patt the rem 139[159] sts; with alt colours, cast on 6 sts (the first st cast on is an edge st, the last 5 sts are steek sts).
Working the steek sts in alt colours and the edge sts in yarn A throughout, at the same time continue to work chart B patt over the back and front sts, until steeks measure 19cm 7½in.

CHART A

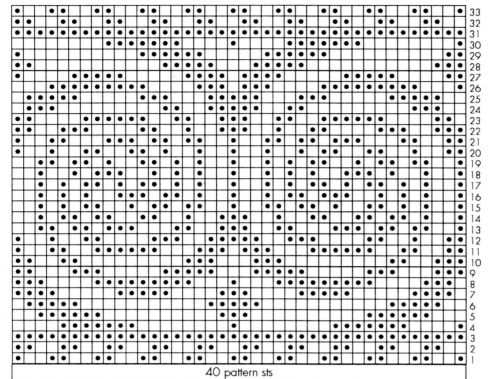

40 pattern sts

KEY

▣ = A
☐ = B

A = 114 [130]cm   A = 45 [51¹/₄]in
B = 67 [69.5]cm   B = 26¹/₂ [27]in
C = 5cm   C = 2in
D = 40 [41]cm   D = 15³/₄ [16¹/₄]in
E = 27 [28.5]cm   E = 10³/₄ [11¹/₄]in
F = 18.5 [21.5]cm F = 7¹/₄ [8¹/₂]in
G = 20 [21]cm   G = 7³/₄ [8¹/₄]in
H = 42 [45.5]cm   H = 16¹/₂ [18]in
I = 27.5 [29]cm   I = 10³/₄ [11¹/₂]in

CHART B

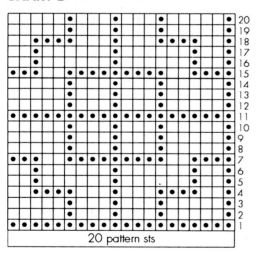

20 pattern sts

KEY

☐ = A
▣ = B

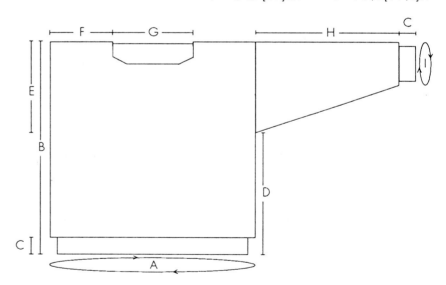

Shape Front Neck

Keeping continuity, k5 steek sts; k1 edge st; patt 59[68] sts; place the next 21[23] sts on a holder; with alt colours, cast on 10 steek sts; patt as set to end of rnd. Work neck steek in alt colours and keeping continuity, dec 1 st at each side of neck steek on next 7 rnds, then on every foll alt rnd 7 times 45[54] chart patt sts rem on

each front shoulder. Patt straight as set for 1 [4] rnds, casting off all steek sts on last rnd. Place centre back 49[51] sts on a holder. With yarn B[A], graft front and back shoulder and edge sts together. With yarn A, sew backstitch up centre of first and last armhole steek sts. Cut open armhole steeks up centre, between 5th and 6th sts.

In 'Armagh' the positive and negative effect of the background grid is accentuated by reversing the border colours.

SLEEVES

With 3¾mm (US5) needles and yarn A, pick up and k the st from safety pin and mark this st; knit up 131[135] sts evenly around armhole, working into the loop of edge st next to chart patt. Work marked st in yarn A throughout and beg at rnd 3[14] of chart B, patt the 131[135] sts as follows:-

Patt the last 5[7] sts of chart B; rep the 20 patt sts 6 times; patt the first 6[8] sts of chart. Keeping continuity of patt, shape sleeve by dec 1 st at each side of marked st on every 4th rnd until 100[86] sts rem, then on every foll 3rd rnd until 68[72] sts rem. AT THE SAME TIME, when 79[88] rnds of chart B have been worked, with 90[92] sts rem, work chart A, setting the patt as follows:-

K marked st in yarn A; patt the last 4[5] sts of chart; rep the 40 patt sts twice; patt the first 5[6] sts of chart. Work the 33 rnds of chart, and keeping continuity, dec as stated.

Next rnd – Dec for Cuff

With yarn A, (k3, k2tog) 2[4] times; (k2, k2tog) 12[8] times; (k3, k2tog) 2[4] times. 52[56] sts. Work 2/2 rib as body for 5cm 2in. With yarn A, cast off knitwise.

FINISHING

NECKBAND

With yarn A, sew backstitch up centre of first and last neck steek sts. Cut open steek up centre, between 5th and 6th sts. With 3¼mm (US3) needles and yarn A, pick up and k the 49[51] sts from back neck holder; knit up 21[23] sts evenly to front holder; pick up and k the 21[23] sts from holder; knit up 21[23] sts to complete rnd. 112[120] sts. Work 2/2 rib as body for 3.5cm 1¼in.

Trim all steeks to 3 sts and with yarn A, cross st in position. Darn in all loose ends. Press lightly on wrong side, omitting all ribs.

The vertical striped ribbed edgings are knitted in the round, with the right side always facing out.

ROSCREA
CELTIC SPIRAL
CHILD'S SWEATER

RATING

★ ★

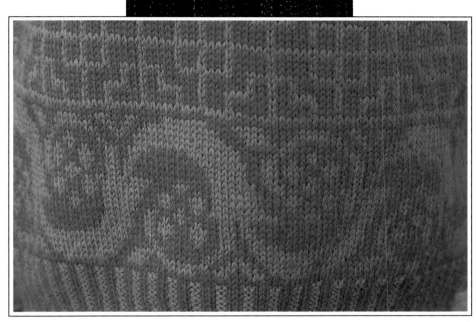

SIZES
To fit age 6-7[10-11] years.
Directions for the larger size are given in parenthesis. Where there is only one set of figures, it applies to both sizes.

KNITTED MEASUREMENTS
Underarm 78[93]cm 30¾[36¾]in.
Length from top of shoulder 43[53]cm 16¾[20¾]in.
Sleeve length 33[41]cm 13[16]in.

MATERIALS
Yarn: Rowan LDK.

A. Pillar Box LDK (45) 225[300]g; **B.** Old Gold LDK (9) 175[225]g.

1 Set of double-pointed or circular 3¼mm (US3) and 3¾mm (US5) needles. 2 Stitch holders. 2 Safety pins. Stitch markers. Darning needle.

A child in 'Roscrea' is partnered here by a companion wearing the 'Rosemarkie' waistcoat (page 23).

For this child's sweater, I have used the same fretwork patterns as Armagh, and a similar border where the spirals are composed of curving horns and sprays of flowers. To soften this image I have chosen the ancient shades of red and gold.

TENSION (GAUGE)
13 sts and 16 rows to 5cm (2in), measured over chart B patt, using 3¾mm (US5) needles.

STITCHES
2/2 rib: K2 with the first colour, p2 with second colour, stranding the yarns evenly across the wrong side. **Chart patt**: K every rnd, and on two-colour rnds, strand the yarn not in immediate use evenly across the wrong side. On stretches of more than 5 sts in one colour, weave in the yarn once at centre of stretch. **Steeks**: Worked at armholes and front neck, and later cut up centre to form openings. The steek is worked over 10 sts. K these sts on every rnd, and on two-colour rnds, k each st and rnd in alt colours. Do not weave in newly joined in or broken off yarns at the centre of armhole steek. Instead leave approx. 5cm 2in tail when joining in and breaking off yarns. **Edge stitch**: Worked at each side of armhole steeks and k in background colour on every rnd. Sts for sleeves are knitted up from edge sts. **Cross stitch**: With darning needle, overcast raw edge of steeks to strands on wrong side of knitting. After sewing to end, reverse to form cross sts (see page 137).

BODY
With 3¼mm (US3) needles and yarn A, cast on 200[240] sts. Place a marker at beg of rnd, and making sure that cast on edge is not twisted, join in yarn B and work k2 A, p2 B rib for 5.5[6.5]cm 2¼[2½]in.

Change to 3¾mm (US5) needles and work the 27 rnds of patt from chart A, repeating

115

CHART A

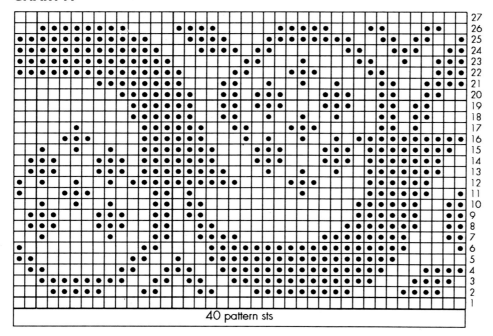

40 pattern sts

CHART B

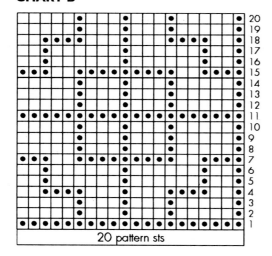

20 pattern sts

KEY

☐ = A
⊡ = B

the 40 patt sts 5[6] times in the rnd. Then work the patt from chart B, repeating the 20 patt sts 10[12] times in the rnd. Rep the 20 rnds of chart B, and work 32[50] rnds. Break off yarns.

Work Armhole Steeks and Edge Sts
Place the first st of rnd on a safety pin; with alt colours, cast on 6 sts (the first 5 cast on are steek sts, the last is an edge st); mark the first st cast on for beg of rnd; keeping continuity of chart B, patt the next 99[119] sts; place the next st on a safety pin; with alt colours, cast on 12 sts (the first and last cast on are edge sts, the centre 10 are steek sts); keeping continuity of chart B, patt the rem 99[119] sts; with alt colours cast on 6 sts (the first cast on is an edge st, the last 5 are steek sts). Work steek sts in alt colours and edge sts in A throughout, and continue to work chart B over front and back sts until 72[98] rnds of chart B have been worked from beg.

Striking autumnal shades of double knitting yarn make this a jolly sweater for a child – and the over-sized shape with a snug neckline is comfortable to wear.

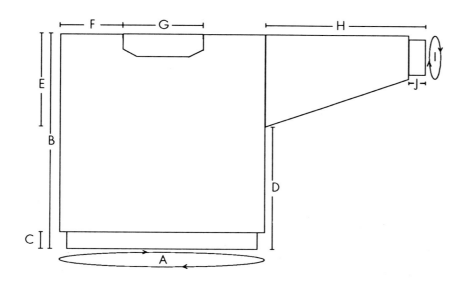

A = 78 [93]cm   30³/₄ [36³/₄]in
B = 43 [53]cm   16³/₄ [20³/₄]in
C = 5.5 [6.5]cm   2¹/₄ [2¹/₂]in
D = 24.5 [30.5]cm   9¹/₂ [12]in
E = 18.5 [22.5]cm   7¹/₄ [8³/₄]in
F = 12 [14.5]cm   4³/₄ [5³/₄]in
G = 15 [18]cm   6 [7]in
H = 33 [41]cm   13 [16]in
I = 21 [24]cm   8¹/₄ [9¹/₂]in
J = 5 [6.5]cm   2 [2¹/₂]

Shape Front Neck
Keeping continuity, k5 steek sts; k1 edge st; patt 41[50] sts; place the next 17[19] sts on a holder; with alt colours, cast on 10 steek sts; patt as set to end of rnd. Work neck steek in alt colours and keeping continuity of patt, dec 1 st at each side of neck steek on next 6 rnds, then on every foll alt rnd 5[7] times. 30[37] chart patt sts rem on each front shoulder. Patt straight for 1 rnd, casting off all steek sts on this rnd. Place centre back 39[45] sts on a holder. With yarn B, graft front and back shoulders and edge sts together.

SLEEVES
With yarn A, sew backstitch up centre of first and last armhole steek sts. Cut open armhole steeks up centre, between 5th and 6th sts.

With 3¼mm (US5) needles and yarn A, pick up and k the st from safety pin and mark this st; knit up 95[115] sts evenly around armhole, working into loop of edge st next to chart patt. Work the marked st in yarn A throughout, and beg at rnd 1 of chart B, set the patt and shape sleeve as follows :-
K the marked st with A; patt the last 7 sts of chart; rep the 20 patt sts 4[5] times; work the first 8 sts of chart. Keeping continuity of patt, dec 1 st at each side of marked st on every 4th rnd. Work 61[81] rnds of chart B in total. 66[76] sts rem. Work chart A, setting the patt as follows:-
K the marked st with A; patt the last 13[18] sts of chart A; work the 40 patt sts once; patt the first 12[17] sts. Work all 27 rnds of chart and keeping continuity of patt continue to dec on every 4th rnd until 54[62] sts rem.

Next Rnd – Dec for Cuff
With yarn A,(k2tog, k4[5]) twice[once]; (k2tog k3[4]) 6[8] times; (k2tog, k4[5]) twice[once]. 44[52] sts.

Change to 3¼mm (US3) needles and work 2/2 rib as body until cuff measures 5 [6.5] cm 2[2½]in. Cast off knitwise with yarn A.

FINISHING

NECKBAND
With yarn A sew backstitch up centre of first and last front neck steek sts. Cut open steek up centre, between 5th and 6th steek sts. With 3¼mm (US3) needles and yarn A, pick up and k the 39 [45] sts from back neck holder; knit up 16[20] sts to front neck holder; pick up and k the 17[19] sts from holder; knit up 16[20] sts to complete rnd. 88[104] sts. Work 2/2 rib as body for 2.5[3.5]cm 1[1½]in. Cast off knitwise with yarn A.

Trim all steeks to 3 sts and with yarn A, cross st in position. Darn in all loose ends. Press lightly on wrong side, omitting all ribs.

Disappearing into the distance these designs are as distinctive from the back as they are from the front.

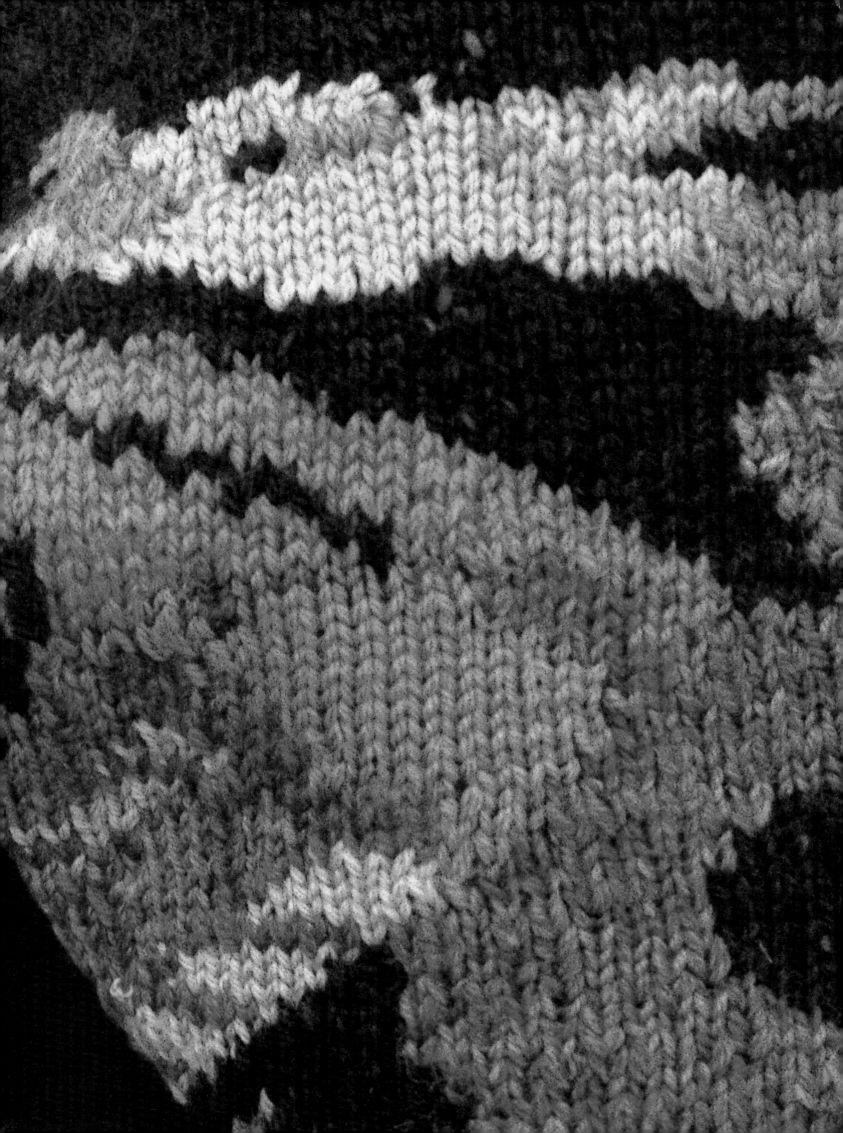

CELTIC CREATURES

ERIN
CARDIGAN
WITH CELTIC
CREATURES

RATING
★ ★ ★ ★

Celtic art is redolent with fabulous and intricately interlaced creatures. For this jacket, I have combined bands of beasts with check patterns and interlaced braids in a warm range of colours to create a challenge for the most experienced knitter.

SIZES

To fit bust 86-91[96-102]cm 32-34[38-40]in.
Directions for larger size are given in parenthesis. Where there is only one set of figures, it applies to both sizes.

KNITTED MEASUREMENTS

Underarm (buttoned) 108[115]cm 42½[45½]in.
Length from top of shoulder 57.5[60.5]cm 22¾[23¾]in.
Sleeve length 47[49]cm 18½[19¼]in.

MATERIALS

Yarn: Rowan Donegal Tweed; Rowan Botany; Rowan Fine Cotton Chenille; Rowan Silkstones.

A. Juniper Donegal Tweed (482) 150[175]g; **B.** Madder Red Botany (45) 50[75]g; **C.** Rust Botany (26) 50g; **D.** Terracotta Botany (526) 25[50]g; **E.** Sienna Botany (104) 50g; **F.** Roseberry Donegal Tweed (480) 75g; **G.** Flamenco Fine Chenille (398) 25g; **H.** Cinnamon Donegal Tweed (479) 75g; **I.** Red Violet Botany (94) 50g; **J.** Old Gold Botany (9) 25g; **K.** Lacquer Fine Chenille (388) 25g; **L.** Jade Botany (100) 25g; **M.** Light Jade Botany (89) 25g; **N.** Blue Mist Silkstones (832) 50g; **O.** Ochre Fine Chenille (401) 25g.

1 Set of double-pointed or circular 3¼mm (US3) needles. 1 Set of double pointed 2¾mm (US2) needles. 3 Stitch holders. 2 Safety pins. Stitch markers. 1 Darning needle. 13[14] buttons.

TENSION (GAUGE)

16 sts and 19 rows to 5cm (2in), measured over chart patt using 3¼mm (US3) needles, and working on right side only, breaking off the yarns at the end of every row. See page 137 for making a Fair Isle swatch.

STITCHES

2/2 rib: K2 with the first colour, p2 with the second colour, stranding the yarns evenly across wrong side. **Chart patt:** K every round, and on two-colour rounds, strand the yarn not in immediate use evenly across wrong side. On stretches of more than 7 sts in one colour, weave in

yarn not in use at centre of stretch. **Steeks:** Worked at centre front, armholes, and neck, and later cut up centre to form openings. The steek is worked over 10 sts. K these sts on every round and on two-colour rounds, k each st and round in alt colours. Do not weave in newly joined or broken off yarns at centre of front steek. Instead leave approx. 5cm (2in) tail when joining in and breaking off yarns. **Edge stitch:** Worked at each side of front and armhole steeks, and k in background colours on every round. Sts for sleeves and front bands are knitted up from edge stitches. **Cross stitch:** With darning needle, overcast raw edge of steeks to strands on wrong side of knitting, and after sewing to end, reverse to form cross stitches. See page 137 for full illustrations of steeks, edge stitches and cross stitch.

BODY

With 3¼mm (US3) needles and H, cast on 338[362] sts. Mark the first st of rnd, and making sure that cast on edge is not twisted, join in and break off colurs as required, and work steeks, edge sts and 2/2 rib as follows:-
Rnds 1 and 2: With alt colours, k5 steek sts; with H, k1 edge st; * k2 H, p2 B; rep from * to the last 8 sts; k2 H; with H, k1 edge st; with alt colours, k5 steek sts.
Rnds 3 and 4: As set, but substituting J for H and H for B. **Rnds 5 and 6:** As set, but substituting H for J and I for H. Repeat these 6 rnds until rib measures 4.5[5]cm 1¾[2]in.

Next rnd – Increase
With F, k5 steek sts; k1 edge st; k81[87]; * m1; k82[88]; rep from * once more; m1; k81[87]; k1 edge st; k5 steek sts. 341[365] sts. **Next rnd:** Join in O and with alt colours, k5 steek sts; with F, k1 edge st;

Knitted in the traditional way on circular needles, 'Erin' is a beautiful cardigan combining several yarns and 15 warm and smoky colours.

CHART A

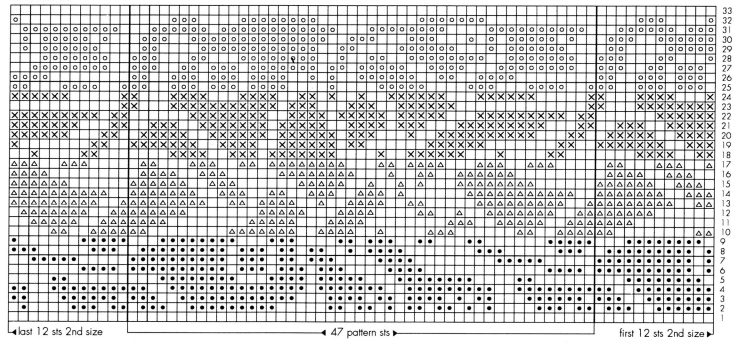

◄ last 12 sts 2nd size | ◄ 47 pattern sts ► | first 12 sts 2nd size ►

CHART B

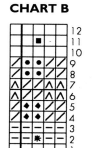

◄ 4 pattern sts
◄ last st

CHART D

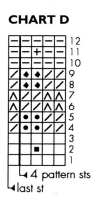

◄ 4 pattern sts
◄ last st

KEY

□ = A
● = B
△ = C
✕ = D
○ = E
⊟ = F
✳ = G
╱ = H
◆ = I
∧ = J
■ = K
∨ = L
▫ = M
Ⴭ = N
⊞ = O

CHART C

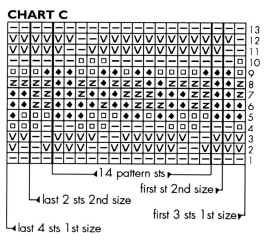

◄ 14 pattern sts
first st 2nd size ►
◄ last 2 sts 2nd size
first 3 sts 1st size ►
◄ last 4 sts 1st size

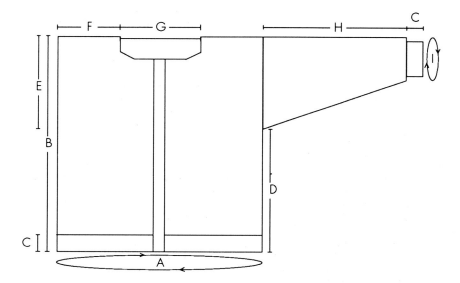

A = 108 [115]cm — 42¹⁄₂ [45¹⁄₂]in
B = 57.5 [60.5]cm — 22³⁄₄ [23³⁄₄]in
C = 4.5 [5]cm — 1³⁄₄ [2]in
D = 33.5 [35.5]cm — 13¹⁄₄ [14]in
E = 24 [25]cm — 9¹⁄₂ [9³⁄₄]in
F = 16.5 [18]cm — 6¹⁄₂ [7]in
G = 19 [21]cm — 7¹⁄₂ [8¹⁄₄]in
H = 42.5 [44]cm — 16³⁄₄ [17¹⁄₄]in
I = 26 [27]cm — 10¹⁄₄ [10³⁄₄]in

k2 F, k1 O; * k3 F, k1 O; rep from * to the last 8 sts; k2 F; with F, k1 edge st; with alt colours, k5 steek sts. Break off O, and with F, k 1 rnd.

Joining in and breaking off colours as required, continue working steek and edge sts as set, and work the patt from chart A, repeating the 47 sts 7 times in the rnd. On 2nd size only, work the first and last 12 sts at beg and end, as indicated. Then, working steek and edge sts as set throughout, work the patts from chart B, then chart C, then chart D, repeating the patt sts and working any sts at beg and end, as indicated. Repeat the sequence of chart A,B,C,D throughout. When 108[114] chart patt rnds have been worked from beg (rnd 5[11] inclusive of chart B), work armholes as follows:-
With colours as for next rnd of chart, k5 steek sts; k1 edge st; patt 81[87] sts; m1 edge st; place the next st on a safety pin; with alt colours, cast on 10 steek sts; m1 edge st; keeping continuity of chart, patt 165[177] sts; m1 edge st; place the next st on a safety pin; with alt colours, cast on 10 steek sts; m1 edge st; keeping continuity of chart, patt 81[87] sts; k1 edge st; k5 steek sts.

Continue as set, working charts in sequence, and working all steeks in alt colours on two-colour rnds, and all edge sts in background colours, until 170[177] chart patt rnds have been worked from beg (rnd 30[4] inclusive of chart A[B]).

Shape Front Neck
With colours as for next rnd of chart, cast off 5 steek sts; k1 edge st; patt the next 10[11] sts and place these sts and edge st on a holder; keeping continuity of chart, work as set to the last 16 [17] sts; patt the next 10[11] sts; k1 edge st and place these last 11[12] sts on a holder; with alt colours, cast off 5 steek sts. Break off yarns.

Next rnd: With alt colours as for next rnd of chart, cast on 5 steek sts; ssk; keeping continuity of chart, work as set to the last 2 sts of rnd; k2tog; with alt colours, cast on 5 steek sts. Mark the first st of rnd and continue as set, working the front neck steek in alt colours, and dec 1 st at each

side of steek on every rnd, until 60[65] chart patt sts rem on each front shoulder. Then dec as set on every foll alt rnd until 52[56] chart patt sts rem on each front shoulder. AT THE SAME TIME, when 190[199] chart patt rnds have been worked from beg (rnd 5[1] inclusive of chart C[D]), shape back neck as follows:-
Working next rnd of chart, continue as set to back chart patt sts. Keeping continuity of chart, patt 56[60] sts; place the next 53[57] sts on a holder; with alt colours, cast on 10 steek sts; keeping continuity of chart, work as set to end of rnd. Work back neck steek in alt colours and keeping continuity of chart, dec 1 st at each side of back neck steek on next and foll alt rnds until 52[56] patt sts rem on each back shoulder. Work straight through rnd 1[10] of chart D, casting off all steek sts on this final rnd.

With A[F], graft shoulder sts together, including edge sts. See page 137 for grafting. With A, sew backstitch up centre of first and last armhole and neck steek sts. Cut open armhole steeks up centre between 5th and 6th sts.

SLEEVES
With 3¼mm (US3) needles and A, pick up and k the st from safety pin and mark this st; then knit up 149[157] sts evenly around armhole, working into loop of edge st next to chart patt. K the marked st in background colours throughout, and shape sleeve by dec 1 st at each side of marked st on every 5th rnd, until 104[120] sts rem, then on every foll 4rd rnd until 82[86] sts rem. AT THE SAME TIME, patt the sleeve in the foll sequence:-
Patt the first 3 rnds of chart D; * work chart C upside down; Chart B upside down: chart A upside down; chart D upside down; rep the sequence from * once more, then work chart C upside down; 3[7] rnds of chart B upside down. With A[H], dec for cuff as follows:-
(K2tog, k3) 5[7] times; (k2tog, k2) 8[4] times; (k2tog, k3) 5[7] times. 64[68] sts. Change to 2¾mm (US2) needles and work 2/2 rib for 4.5[5]cm 1¾[2]in, in colours as body, from top of rib to cast on edge. With H, cast off knitwise.

NECKBAND
Cut open front and neck steeks up centre, between 5th and 6th sts.
With right side facing, 2¾mm (US2) needles, and H, pick up and k the 11[12] sts from right front holder; knit up 35[36] sts evenly to back neck holder; pick up and k the 53[57] sts from holder and dec 1 st at centre; knit up 35[36] sts to left front holder; pick up and k the 11[12] sts from holder. 144[152] sts.
Work 2 /2 rib as follows:-
Row 1: With J, p1 edge st; * p2 J, k2 H; rep from * to the last 3 sts; p2 J; with J, p1 edge st.
Row 2: With J, k1 edge st; * k2 J, p2 H; rep from * to the last 3 sts; k2 J; with J, k1 edge st.
Rows 3 and 4: As rows 1 and 2, but substituting H for J, and B for H.
Rows 5 and 6: As set, but substituting I for B.
Rows 7 and 8: As rows 1 and 2.
Rows 9 and 10: As rows 3 and 4.
With H, cast off loosely and evenly, knitwise.

LEFT FRONT BAND
With right side facing, 2¾mm (US2) needles and H, knit up 158[166] sts, evenly along right front edge, working into loop of edge st next to chart patt. Work 10 rows of 2/2 rib in colours as neckband, beg and ending wrong side rows with p2, and right side rows with k2. With H, cast off loosely and evenly, knitwise.

RIGHT FRONT BAND
As left, with the addition of 13[14] buttonholes to be worked on 6th row, as follows:-
First size: Rib 3; * cast off 2, rib 11, cast off 2, rib 10; rep from * 6 times; cast off 2, rib 3.
2nd Size: Rib 4; * cast off 2, rib 10; rep from * 13 times; cast off 2, rib 4.
Next row – both sizes: Rib as set, casting on 2 sts over those cast off.
Complete rib following instructions for left front band. With H, cast off.

FINISHING
Trim all steeks to 3 sts and cross st in position. Darn in all loose ends. Press lightly on wrong side, omitting ribs. Sew on buttons.

TIPPERARY
CHILD'S SWEATER
WITH CELTIC CREATURES

RATING
★ ★ ★

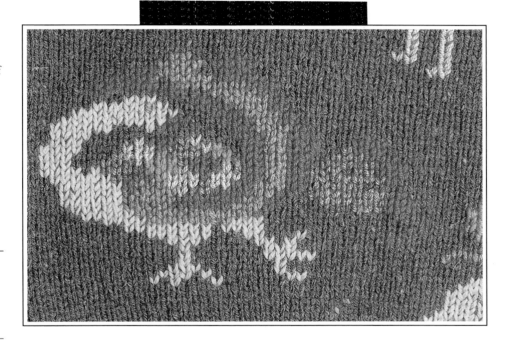

SIZES
To fit age 4-5[6-7,8-9] years.
Directions for larger sizes are given in parenthesis. Where there is only one set of figures, it applies to all sizes.

KNITTED MEASUREMENTS
Underarm 76[82,90]cm 30[32½, 35½]in.
Length from top of shoulder 38[40,42]cm 15[15¾,16½]in.
Sleeve length 29[31.5,34]cm 11½[12½,13½]in.

MATERIALS
Yarn: Rowan Donegal Tweed; Silk/Wool; Botany.

A. Juniper Donegal Tweed (482) 300[325,350]g; **B.** Royal Blue Silk/Wool (848) 20g; **C.** Purple Silk/Wool (841) 20g; **D.** Fuchsia Silk/Wool (843) 20g; **E.** Madder Red Botany (45) 25g; **F.** Gold Botany (525) 25g; **G.** Leaf Green Botany (605) 25g; **H.** Pale Yellow Botany (6) 25g.

Note: All yarns are used doubled throughout.

1 Pair each 3¾mm (US5) and 4½mm (US7) needles. 2 Stitch holders. Stitch markers. Darning needle.

TENSION (GAUGE)
21 sts and 30 rows to 10cm (4in), measured over st.st., using 4½mm (US7) needles and yarn A doubled.

STITCHES
Chart Patt: Worked entirely in st.st. Odd numbered rows are right side, even numbered rows are wrong side. Use separate lengths of yarn for each area of colour. Link one colour to the next by twisting them around each other where

Every child will love this sweater with four mythical figures that appear on the front, back and sleeves. It is worked throughout in double yarn to give extra warmth.

they meet on the wrong side to avoid gaps. See page 137 for intarsia knitting. The main and all contrast yarns are used doubled throughout e.g. AA means use two strands of A, BB means use two strands of B etc.

BACK
** With 3¾mm (US5) needles and AA, cast on 74[78,82] sts. Work mock cable rib as follows:-
Rows 1 and 3 (wrong side): K2, * p2, k2; rep from * to end of row. **Row 2**: P2, * k2, p2; rep from * to end of row. **Row 4**: P2, * k2tog and leave sts on left hand needle; insert right hand needle between the 2 sts knitted together and k the first st again; slip both sts from needle together;

One of my favourite aspects of the Book of Kells is the menagerie of fantastic, acrobatic little creatures which inhabit almost every page of text, sometimes curled into the initial letter of a sentence, but almost as often just filling a space. They have an undoubted aura of fun and mischief which makes them perfect images for a child's sweater. Here I have used four figures at random on the back and front of this design.

p2; rep from * to end of row.
Rep these 4 rows once more, then work rows 1 and 2.

Next Row – Increase
Rib 1[3,1], * m1, rib 18[12,8]; rep from * to the last 1[3,1] sts; m1, rib 1[3,1]. 79[85,93] sts.

Change to 4½mm (US7) needles and work patt from chart until back measures 20.5[20.5,21]cm 8[8,8¼]in from cast on edge. *** Place a marker at each end of row and continue working chart through row 96[102,110].

Shape Neck and Shoulders
Continue working from chart and patt

CHART A

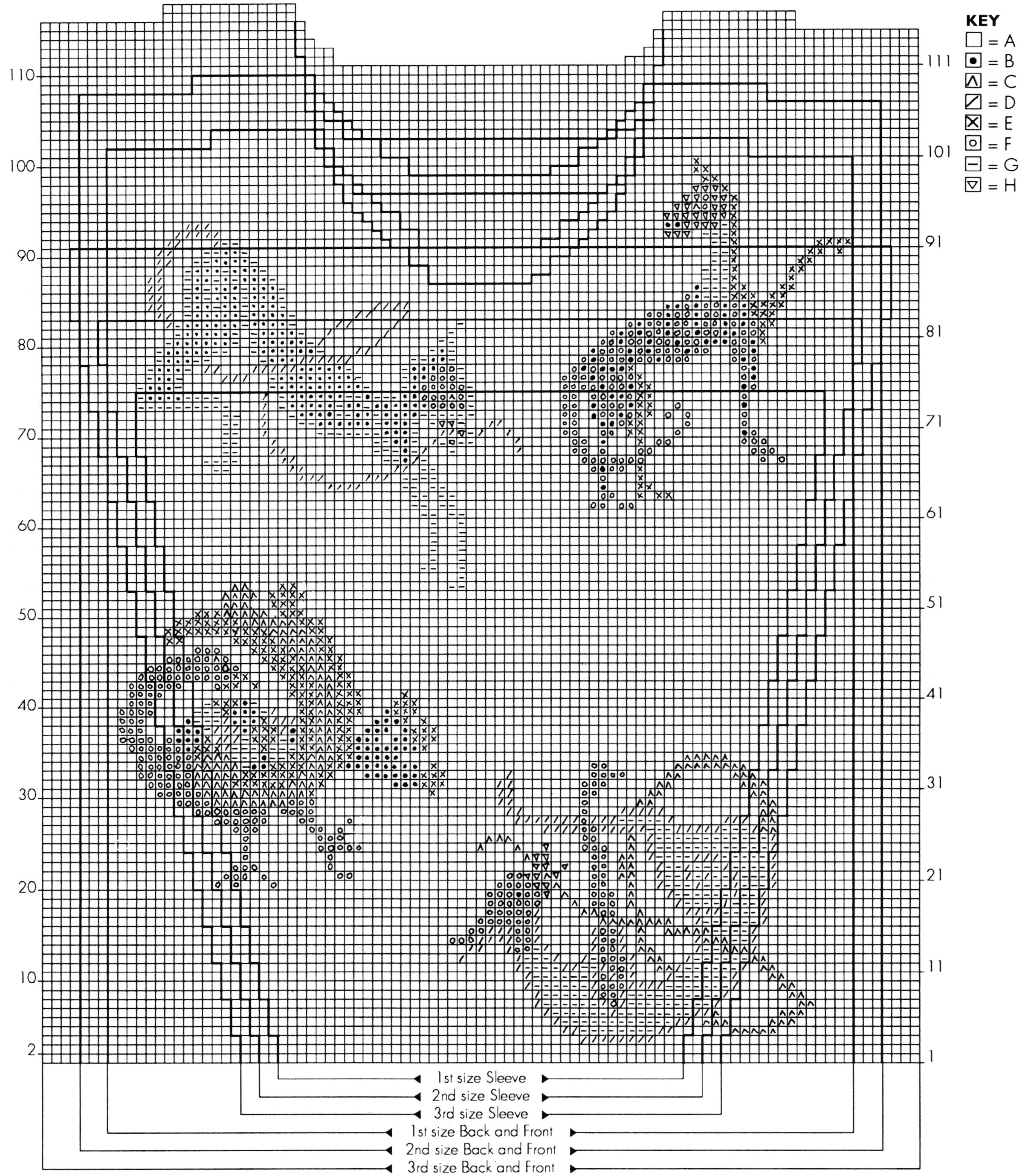

KEY

☐ = A
⊡ = B
△ = C
⧄ = D
⊠ = E
⊙ = F
⊟ = G
▽ = H

◄ 1st size Sleeve ►
◄ 2nd size Sleeve ►
◄ 3rd size Sleeve ►
◄ 1st size Back and Front ►
◄ 2nd size Back and Front ►
◄ 3rd size Back and Front ►

The figures on this sweater are knitted using the intarsia technique where small, separate balls of yarn are required for individual motifs.

26[28,31] sts; leave the rem sts on a spare needle. Turn and work right side as follows:-
Row 1: Cast off 2, patt to end of row.
Row 2: Patt to the last 2 sts, k2tog. **Row 3**: Patt straight. **Row 4**: Cast off 11[12,13]; patt to the last 2 sts; k2tog. Patt 1 row straight, then cast off the rem 11[12,14] sts. With right side facing, place the first 27[29,31] sts from spare needle on a holder; rejoin yarn and patt 2 rows straight. Then shape neck and shoulder as right side, reversing shapings as indicated on chart.

FRONT
As back from ** to ***. Place a marker at each end of row and continue working chart patt through row 86[90,98].

Shape Neck and Shoulders
Continue working from chart and patt 34[36,39] sts; leave the rem sts on a spare needle. Turn and shape left side as follows:-

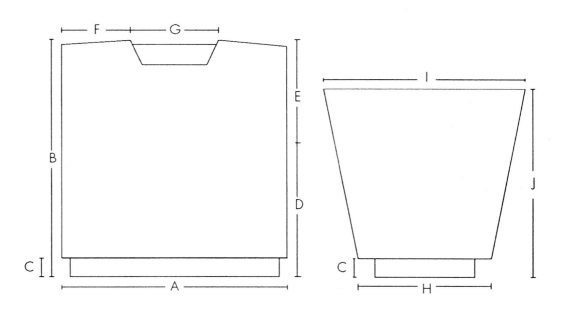

A = 38 [41, 45]cm
B = 38 [40, 42]cm
C = 4cm
D = 20.5 [20.5, 21]cm
E = 17.5 [19.5, 21]cm
F = 10.5 [11.5, 13]cm
G = 17 [18, 19]cm
H = 21 [23, 25]cm
I = 35 [39, 42]cm
J = 29 [31.5, 34]cm

A = 15 [16¼, 17¾]in
B = 15 [15¾, 16½]in
C = 1½in
D = 8 [8, 8¼]in
E = 7 [7¾, 8¼]in
F = 4¼ [4½, 5¼]in
G = 6½ [7, 7¼]in
H = 8¼ [9, 9¾]in
I = 14 [15½, 16½]in
J = 11½ [12½, 13½]in

'Tipperary' is led here by 'Kilronan', a tunic-style sweater with knotwork patterns (see page 91).

Cast off 2[2,3] sts at beg of next row. Patt 1 row straight. Cast off 2 sts at beg of next row. Dec 1 st at neck edge of next 5 rows, then at neck edge of every foll alt row 3[3,2] times. When front corresponds in length with back at shoulder, with right side facing for next row, shape shoulder by casting off 11[12,13] sts at beg of row. Patt 1 row straight, then cast off the rem 11[12,14] sts.

With right side facing, place the first 11[13,15] sts from spare needle on a holder. Rejoin yarn to the rem 34[36,39] sts and patt 2 rows straight. Then shape neck and shoulder as left side, reversing shapings as indicated on chart.

SLEEVES
With 3¾mm (US5) needles and AA, cast on 34[38,42] sts. Work mock cable rib as back for 10 rows.

Next Row – Increase
Rib 1[3,1], * m1, rib 4[4,5]; rep from * to the last 1[3,1] sts; m1, rib 1[3,1]. 43[47,51] sts.

Change to 4½mm (US7) needles and work patt from chart increasing 1 st at each end of every 4th row 7 times, then at each end of every foll 5th row until there are 73[81,87] sts, as indicated on chart. Continue straight in patt for 6[4,7] rows. With AA, cast off evenly.

FINISHING
Press all pieces lightly on wrong side,

omitting ribs. Join back and front at left shoulder seam.

NECKBAND
With right side facing, 3¾mm (US5) needles and AA, knit up 6 sts evenly to back neck holder; pick up and k the 27[29,31] sts from holder; knit up 22[24,26] sts evenly to front holder; pick up and k the 11[13,15] sts from holder; knit up 16[18,20] sts evenly to shoulder cast off. 82[90,98] sts. Work 6 rows of mock cable rib as back. Cast off neatly and evenly in rib.

Join right shoulder and neckband seam. Place centre top of sleeves at shoulder seams and sew sleeves to body between markers. Press seams lightly on wrong side, omitting neckband rib. Sew up side and sleeve seams and press seams lightly on wrong side, omitting ribs.

SHANNON
CHILD'S JACKET
WITH CELTIC CREATURES

RATING

SIZES
To fit age 5-6[7-8] years.
Directions for larger size are given in parenthesis. Where there is only one set of figures, it applies to both sizes.

KNITTED MEASUREMENTS
Underarm (buttoned) 76[82]cm 30[32½]in.
Length from top of shoulder 38[40.5]cm 15[16¼]in.
Sleeve length 29[31.5]cm 11½[12½]in.

MATERIALS
Yarn: Rowan Lambswool Tweed; Donegal Tweed; Botany.

Main. Dark Ore Lambswool (183) 5[6] 50g balls; **A.** Jade Botany (100) 25g; **B.** Turquoise Botany (528) 25g; **C.** Madder Red Botany (45) 25g; **D.** Rust Botany (26) 25g; **E.** Old Gold Botany (9) 25g; **F.** Green Gold Botany (405) 25g; **G.** Straw Botany (664) 25g; **H.** Juniper Donegal (482) 25g; **I.** Leaf Donegal (481) 25g; **J:** Roseberry Donegal (480) 25g; **K.** Cinnamon Donegal (479) 25g.

1 Pair each 3¼mm (US3) and 3¾mm (US5) needles. Stitch markers. 1 Darner. 5 Buttons.

TENSION (GAUGE)
24 sts and 32 rows to 10cm (4in), measured over st.st. using 3¾mm (US5) needles.

STITCHES
Chart patt: Worked entirely in st.st. Odd numbered rows are right side, even numbered rows are wrong side. Use separate lengths of yarn for each area of colour. Link one colour to the next by twisting them around each other where they meet on the wrong side, to avoid gaps. See page 137 for intarsia knitting. All contrast yarns are used in combination throughout e.g. AI means use 1 strand of A and one strand of I.

BACK
With 3¼mm (US3) needles and main yarn, cast on 80[84] sts. Work k1, p1 rib for 6[7]cm 2½[2¾]in.

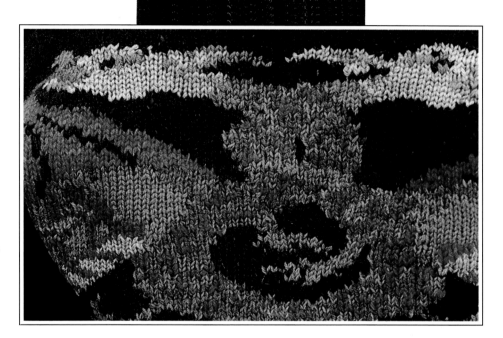

Fiery interlaced dragons with floreated tails are engraved on the silver casing of the Clogan Oir (little bell of gold). The bell has long been associated with St Senan, who was the founder of the monastery on Scattery Island, in the estuary of the river Shannon in Ireland. For this child's jacket, guaranteed to make an impact especially from behind, I used the dark expanse of the back to display the dramatic colourful dragons. The fronts and sleeves are scattered with bright snowflake-type motifs.

Next row – Increase
Rib 5[6]; * m1, rib 7[6]; rep from * to the last 5[6] sts; m1, rib 5[6]. 91[97] sts. Change to 3¾mm (US5) needles, and joining in and breaking off colours as required, work the patt from chart A until back measures 20[21.5]cm 8[8½]in from cast on edge. Place a marker at each end of row and continue working chart A through row 100[106].

Shape Shoulders
Cast off 9[10] sts at beg of next 4 rows. Cast off 10 sts at beg of next 2 rows. Cast off the rem 35[37] sts.

RIGHT FRONT
With 3¼mm (US3) needles and main yarn, cast on 36[40] sts. Work rib as back for 6[7]cm 2½[2¾]in.

Next row – Increase
Rib 3[2]; * m1, rib 6[9]; rep from * to the last 3[2] sts; m1, rib 3[2]. 42[45] sts.

Change to 3¾mm (US5) needles, and joining in and breaking off colours as required, work the patt from chart B through row 68[70].

Shape Neck
Cast off 3 sts at beg of next row. Dec 1 st

CHART A – BACK

KEY

⊟ = AI	⊡ = EE
◸ = BH	⋀ = FF
■ = DK	☒ = GG
• = CJ	◿ = BB
	⋁ = AA

(Follow inner black lines for first size and outer black lines for second size)

Viewed from the front, 'Shannon' is a delightful design for a child. The comfortable jacket shape, with its ribbed revers collar, is studded with bright motifs.

CHART C – LEFT FRONT　　　　　　　　　　**CHART B – RIGHT FRONT**

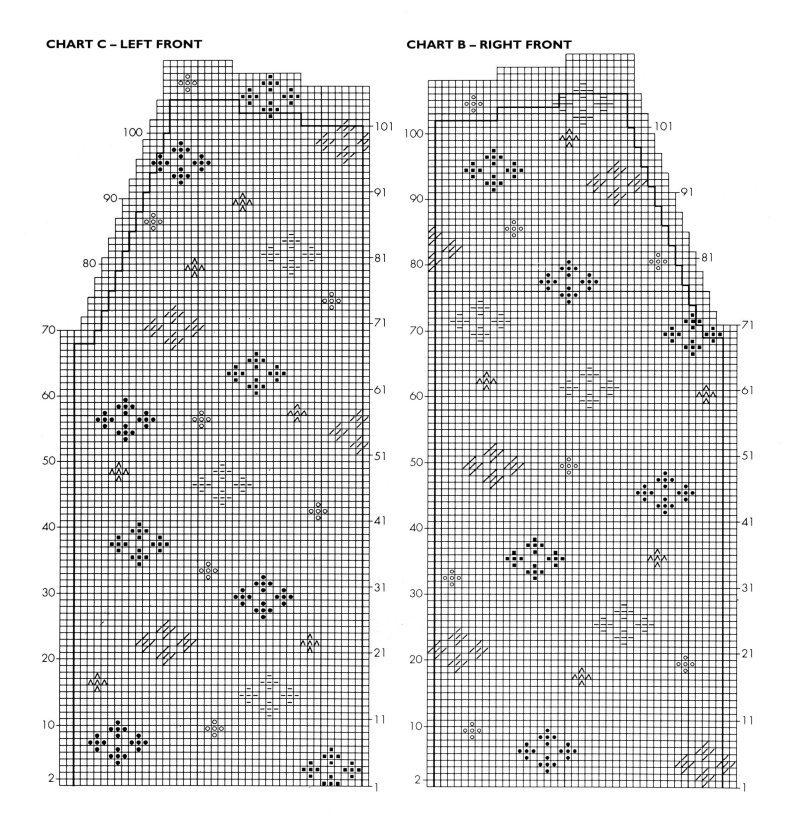

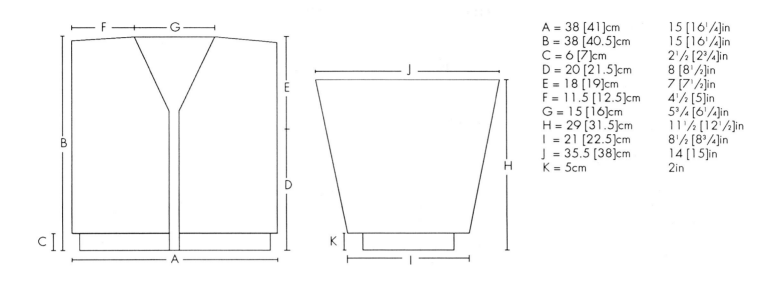

A = 38 [41]cm   15 [16¹/₄]in
B = 38 [40.5]cm   15 [16¹/₄]in
C = 6 [7]cm   2¹/₂ [2³/₄]in
D = 20 [21.5]cm   8 [8¹/₂]in
E = 18 [19]cm   7 [7¹/₂]in
F = 11.5 [12.5]cm   4¹/₂ [5]in
G = 15 [16]cm   5³/₄ [6¹/₄]in
H = 29 [31.5]cm   11¹/₂ [12¹/₂]in
I = 21 [22.5]cm   8¹/₂ [8³/₄]in
J = 35.5 [38]cm   14 [15]in
K = 5cm   2in

CHART D – SLEEVE

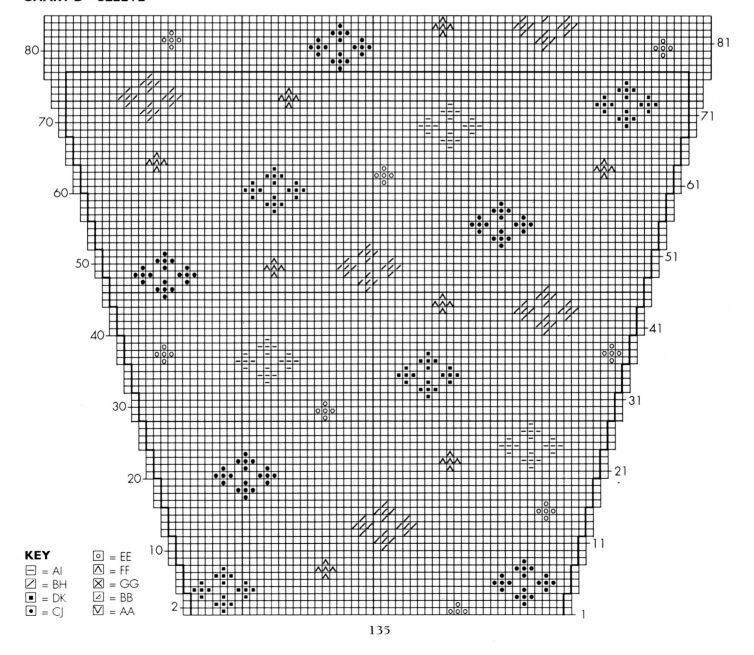

KEY

⊟ = AI   ⊡ = EE
⊘ = BH   ⅄ = FF
▪ = DK   ⊠ = GG
⊡ = CJ   ⊿ = BB
       ⊽ = AA

Seen here with 'Kells' (page 51), the back of 'Shannon' shows the colourful and dramatic dragon design in its full glory.

at neck edge of next alt row, then every foll 3rd row until 28[30] sts rem. Patt 0[1] row straight.

Shape Shoulder
Cast off 9[10] sts at beg of next and foll alt row. Work 1 row straight, then cast off the rem 10 sts.

Place a marker at armhole edge to correspond with marker on back.

LEFT FRONT
As right front, but working patt from chart C through row 67[69]. Shape neck and shoulders as right front, reversing shapings as indicated on chart.

Place a marker at armhole edge to correspond with marker on back.

SLEEVES
With 3¼mm (US3) needles and main yarn, cast on 44 sts. Work k1, p1 rib for 5cm 2in.

Next Row – Increase
Rib 1[2]; * m1, rib 7[5]; rep from * to the last 1[2] sts; m1, rib 1[2]. 51[53] sts.

Change to 3¾mm (US5) needles, and joining in and breaking off colours as required, work the patt from chart D and increase 1 st at each end of every 4th row as indicated on chart, until there are 85[91] sts.
Patt the last 8 rows straight from chart. Cast off all sts.

FINISHING
Darn in all loose ends. Press all pieces lightly on wrong side, omitting ribs. Join back and fronts at shoulder seams and press seams lightly on wrong side. Place centre top of sleeves at shoulder seams and sew sleeves to body between markers. Press seams lightly on wrong side. Sew up side and sleeve seams and press seams lightly on wrong side omitting ribs.

BUTTON BAND
With 3¼mm (US3) needles and main yarn, knit up 68[70] sts along left front edge for girl, from beg of neck shaping to cast on edge. Knit up along right front edge for boy, from cast on edge to beg of neck

shaping. K1, p1 rib for 10 rows. Cast off evenly.

BUTTONHOLE BAND
As button band, with the addition of 5 buttonholes to be worked on the 5th row as follows:-
Rib 3[2] * cast off 2, rib 13[14]; rep from * to the last 5[4] sts; cast off 2, rib 3[2]. On the foll row, cast on 2 sts over those cast off in previous row.

COLLAR
With 3¼mm needles (US3) needles and main yarn, cast on 115[125] sts. K1, p1 rib, beg and ending right side rows with k1, and wrong side rows with p1, for 10 rows. Continue in rib and cast off 3 sts at beg of the next and every foll row until 61[65] sts rem. Cast off the rem sts.

Place centre of cast off edge of collar at centre back neck and sew cast off edge of collar along neckline evenly, so that cast on edge of collar and cast off edge of front bands form a continuous line. Sew ends of collar to end of front bands. Sew on buttons to correspond with buttonholes.

KNITTING TECHNIQUES

All patterns in this book contain general information (Sizes, Materials, Tension), written and/or charted instructions and details of how to assemble the garment. Everything is presented in a logical order, but it is important that you read the pattern through before you start knitting so that you have a general understanding of the work.

The information here relates to reading the patterns section by section and describes the techniques that are used consistently.

SIZES
The patterns are usually written in a range of sizes; instructions for the first size are given outside a set of square brackets, [ ], with the larger sizes following on in order within the brackets.

Look at the *actual* measurement when choosing the size to make. Some garments have a generous amount of 'ease', so you may prefer to knit a smaller size than normal if the finished result is too large for your taste. Once you have decided on a size, mark the relevant figures throughout the pattern to avoid confusion.

MATERIALS
In this book the designs are all knitted in Rowan yarns – the names and shades of which are quoted with the individual instructions. To avoid the frustration of being unable to obtain specific yarns, there is a table of generic equivalents (any standard 4 ply, double knitting, etc) on page 143. Only substitute a different yarn after first making a tension swatch and checking that the number of stitches and rows is the same as the original.

Changing yarns could mean that you will need more or less yarn than stated in the pattern, even though both yarns may be packaged in the same weight balls. Due to the composition of the fibres, each type of yarn has a different metreage (yardage) – the actual length of yarn in each ball. Therefore the actual amounts quoted in the pattern can only be used as a guide. Many of the designs in this book use a number of different colours, some in very small quantities. Yarns are frequently only available in 50g (2oz) balls which means that there is a lot left over. If you do a lot

of colourwork knitting, extra yarn may be welcome for future projects. However, keep a scrap box of suitable yarns in colours that you like. It is also possible to buy tapestry yarns in small amounts and a wide range of colours.

TENSION
The tension quoted in a pattern has been achieved by the designer of the garment who uses it to make all the stitch and row calculations. As the tension of your work is personal to you, and to ensure that your

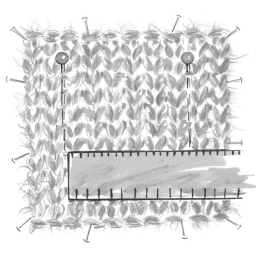

Measuring the stitch tension.

sweater finishes up the size that you intended, you *must* make a tension swatch before starting work.

For intarsia or textured designs, use the yarn and needles stated and working in the appropriate stitch or pattern, knit a swatch about 15cm (6in) square. To make a Fair Isle swatch, see page 137. Place the finished swatch on a padded surface, gently smooth it into shape, then secure the edges with pins placed at right angles to the fabric.

With pins as markers at each end, measure out 10cm (4in) horizontally across the centre of the swatch for the stitch tension, or vertically down the swatch for the row tension. Fewer stitches than stated means

that your work is too loose and you need to try again with smaller needles; more stitches than stated indicates that you are knitting too tightly and should try again with larger needles. Changing the needle size is not important as long as you obtain the correct number of stitches and rows to 10cm (4in).

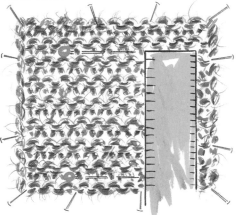

Measuring the row tension.

FAIR ISLE KNITTING
Many of the designs in this book involve the Fair Isle knitting technique. It is a method well worth becoming acquainted with, as it is the fastest and easiest way of knitting colour patterns. The instructions given for each design are specific and detailed, and so the following descriptions and illustrations give a general picture of the techniques which all Fair Isle designs have in common.

All Fair Isle designs are worked in circular fashion, either on double-pointed or circular needles. The main advantage of circular knitting is that the right side of the work is always facing, so that you can see the pattern at all times. This also means that the pattern is worked in knit stitches only. Extra stitches are worked at any openings, such as a cardigan front, armholes and neck, so that the entire garment can be worked in a circle. These extra stitches, called steeks, are later cut up the centre to form the required openings. The garments are also seamless. The shoulder stitches are grafted together

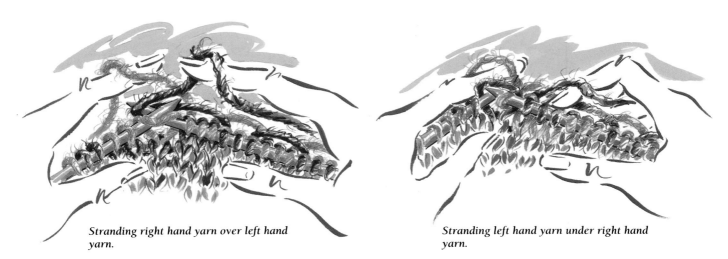

Stranding right hand yarn over left hand yarn.

Stranding left hand yarn under right hand yarn.

and the sleeves are worked by picking up stitches around the armhole and knitting down to the cuff.

Stranded Knitting

A maximum of two colours are used in any one round, with the colour not in immediate use being stranded across the back of the work. It is important to strand the yarn evenly across the back. Strands which are too loose will produce uneven stitches, and stranding too tightly will cause the knitting to pucker.

Most knitters are taught either the 'English' method where the yarn is held in the right hand, or the 'Continental' method where the yarn is held in the left hand. Although either method can be used for stranded knitting, the ideal way to work is by using both, i.e. knitting with a yarn in each hand. By doing this you will avoid having to drop one colour to pick up the

second. The right-hand yarn always crosses over the left-hand yarn, and the left-hand yarn always crosses underneath the right-hand yarn. This means that the two yarns will never twist together and become entangled. Indeed, if you work with one hand only, twisting the yarns can be avoided if you consistently cross one colour over and the other colour under, for the duration of each round.

Occasionally there may be a stretch of more than seven stitches in one colour, and to avoid a long strand it is advisable to weave in the yarn at the centre of the stretch.

Steeks

Steek is the common term used to describe the extra stitches which are worked at openings, in order that knitting may proceed in the round. In all the Fair Isle designs in this book there are 10 extra

stitches worked at all openings. The beginning of the round is always placed at the centre of the first steek to be worked. In the case of a cardigan, this will be at the centre of the front steek which begins at the cast on edge.

On a pullover sweater, the beginning of the round is placed at the centre of the first underarm and then at the centre of the first armhole steek. This means that when the steek is cut open up the centre, all the yarn ends joined in and broken off can be trimmed and discarded, thus avoiding darning them in.

On all two-colour rounds, the steek stitches are knit in alternating colours on every stitch and round, as shown in the drawing. This helps to lock the yarns within the steek. Because many of the yarns used in the designs are very smooth, it is advisable to sew backstitch along the first and last steek stitches before cutting the steek. Do not use a sewing machine as it has a tendency to distort the knitting and forms too rigid a seam. Instead, use very sharp scissors to cut up the centre of each steek, between the fifth and sixth stitches, to that there will be five steek stitches at each side of the opening. The stitches will not run appreciably.

Once you have completed the knitting, the steeks must be finished off. To do this, trim the steeks to a two or three stitch width and immediately cross stitch them in position. Begin at the bottom and overcast the steek, catching into the strands all the way up. Then work downwards, not catching the strands, but aiming to cover the raw edges and forming cross stitches.

Edge Stitches

Edge stitches are worked at each side of front openings of cardigans and at dropped shoulder armholes. The illustration of a steek shows the edge stitches worked at each side of a front steek. Front bands and sleeve stitches are picked up from the edge stitch, thus leaving the steek stitches on one side and the patterned stitches on the other. The edge stitch is always worked in the background colours, so that it is easily distinguished between the steek and the patterned stitches.

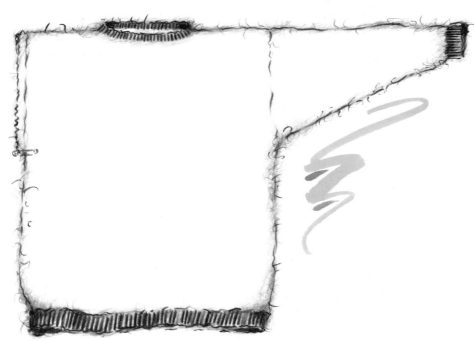

Method of circular Fair Isle knitting.

Weaving in a strand.

Working a steek.

Grafting

On Fair Isle designs, the shoulder stitches are grafted together to avoid seams. Thread a darning needle with the background or dominant colour and graft the stitches together as shown, gently pulling the thread as you go along, until the new set of loops formed are equal in size to those of the knitting. Darn in both yarn ends on completion.

Knitting a Fair Isle Swatch

Just as with all designs, it is vital to knit a Fair Isle swatch, in order to determine the correct tension before you begin the garment. All Fair Isle patterns are worked using knit stitches only, which have a slightly different tension than purl

Finishing a steek.

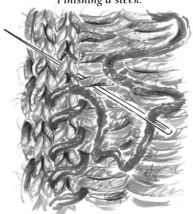

(stage 1)

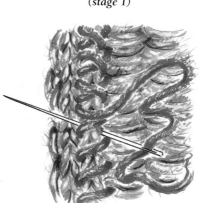

(stage 2)

stitches. It is therefore necessary to knit a swatch in the pattern, using only knit stitches. A circular swatch would have to be very large to give an accurate measurement, and so the best method is to cast on stitches on either a double-pointed or circular needle. Then work the first row of the chart, and break off the yarns at the end of the row. Slide the stitches to the other end of the needle and work the next row, from the right.

Repeat this process, breaking off the yarns at the end of every row. If you find that the first and last stitches are very loose, just give them a good tug or tie the ends together at the beginning and end of the rows. On completion, gently block and press the swatch, and measure the tension.

Reading a Fair Isle Chart

The patterns repeat over a specific number of stitches and rounds. One repeat of the pattern is shown on the chart, which is to be repeated as given in the instructions. One square represents one stitch, and one row of squares represents one round of knitting. All rounds are read from the right, beginning at the bottom with round 1.

INTARSIA

Some designs in this book involve intarsia knitting which is a form of creating colour patterns, usually against a background of stocking stitch. To show how the design evolves, sections of a garment are often presented as charts.

Charts are based on a grid of squares; reading horizontally across the grid each square represents a stitch, and vertically up the grid squares indicate the rows of knitting. Symbols represent the various colours. If you find it difficult to 'read' the symbols, photocopy the chart and shade the squares in the appropriate colours. It is also possible to enlarge a chart if the grid is too small by using the special facility on a photocopier.

Solid lines show the markings for various sizes as well as indicating shaping such as armholes or neck. Only use the lines as a guide for placing the pattern; always follow the written detailed instructions for shaping.

When working an isolated area of colour or a motif, use a separate length of yarn or wind off a small ball (depending on the size of the motif) for each area of colour. It is important to link each colour to the next by twisting the yarns together on the wrong side of the work when you change colour – otherwise the different areas of colour will separate.

MAKING UP

After the many hours that it takes to complete a knitted garment, do not spoil the finished effect by rushing the final

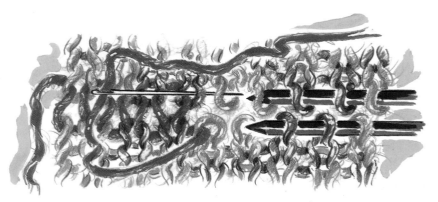

Grafting stitches together.

stages. First make sure that all the loose ends of yarn are secured to prevent them unravelling later on. Always leave a long end of yarn for darning in when you start a new ball of yarn. Thread the end into a blunt-ended wool needle and neatly weave it into the back of the knitting behind the stitches of the same colour. Trim the loose end close to the fabric.

For sewing up intarsia and textured garments, use matching yarn in the main colour and a blunt-ended wool needle. If the original yarn is unsuitable for sewing up (i.e. too thick or textured), choose a similar colour in a finer, smooth quality.

Blocking and Pressing

For a perfect fit, the finished pieces of knitting should be blocked (i.e. pinned out to the measurements indicated in the diagrams) and pressed according to the specific instructions given on the yarn label. Blocking requires a padded surface. Lay a folded blanket on a table and cover it with a sheet. Place the knitted pieces right side down on the sheet and smooth them out to the correct measurements. Check that the fabric is not distorted and that the lines of stitches and rows are straight, then secure to the pad using pins placed at right angles to the edge of the knitting. For most natural fibres, cover the knitting with a damp cloth and, using a warm iron, place it gently onto the fabric and lift it up again – without moving the iron in a continuous action. Allow the knitting to dry completely before removing the pins. Do not press any areas of ribbing or

Linking yarns when changing colour.

stitchwork patterns where the texture of the knitting can easily be damaged. For a Fair Isle garment, press lightly on the wrong side, using a sleeve board for the sleeves.

Backstitch Seam

The most popular seam in common use, the backstitch seam, gives a strong, firm finish to most edges, but forms a ridge on the inside of the garment. To work the seam, place the pieces to be joined with right sides together, matching any patterns row for row and stitch for stitch. Work in backstitch along the seam, close to the edge, sewing into the centre of each row or stitch to correspond with the row or stitch on the opposite edge.

Invisible Seam

This is a very useful seam for working with thick yarns where a backstitch seam would be too bulky. The seam is virtually undetectable from the right side of the work – the only sign is a slight ridge on the inside of the garment. Place the pieces to be joined edge to edge with the right sides facing upwards. By sewing under the horizontal strands (linking the edge stitch and the following stitch) of alternate edges, the two pieces are gradually 'laced' together from the right side.

Overcast Seam

Although the seam is worked through two edges placed together, when it is opened out it lies completely flat. Use an overcast seam for areas of ribbing such as welts and cuffs, or for attaching front bands and collars. With the right sides of the two pieces to be joined together and matching stitches and rows, insert the needle behind the knot of the edge stitch on one side, then through the same part of the corresponding stitch on the second side. Draw the yarn through and repeat these actions to join each pair of row ends.

CARE OF HAND KNITTING

The majority of yarns used in this book are made up of natural fibres; all of them can be hand-washed or dry-cleaned in certain solvents. For further guidance, follow the washing instructions printed on the ball bands or labels.

Hand-washing

Use hand-warm water in which a mild soap has been dissolved. Never allow the garment to soak, or rub it in the water, as the fabric will become felted. Instead, gently squeeze the knitting, supporting it all the time so that the weight of the water does not pull the garment out of shape. Rinse in several changes of water until there is no trace of soap, then spin dry for a short time only.

Never tumble dry a knitted garment or hang it up to dry. Smooth the garment gently into shape and leave it to dry on a flat surface covered with a towel.

Machine-washing

It is possible to machine-wash some cotton yarns on a gentle cycle, but always refer to the instructions with the yarn.

HINTS FOR AMERICAN KNITTERS

The patterns in this book should be easy for American knitters to follow. In case of difficulties the following tables and glossaries offer guidance.

TERMINOLOGY

UK	US
cast off	bind off
cont without shaping	work straight
colour	shade
ball band	yarn label
slip stitch in position	tack down
stocking stitch	stockinette stitch
tension	gauge

The following table shows the approximate yarn equivalents in terms of thickness. Always check the tension of substitute yarns before buying sufficient to complete the garment.

UK	US
four-ply	sport
double knitting	knitting worsted
Aran-weight	fisherman
chuncky	bulky

METRIC CONVERSION TABLES

Length (to the nearest ¹/₄ in)				Weight (rounded up to the nearest ¹/₄ oz)	
cm	in	cm	in	g	oz
1	½	55	21¾	25	1
2	¾	60	23½	50	2
3	1¼	65	25½	100	3¾
4	1½	70	27½	150	5½
5	2	75	29½	200	7¼
6	2½	80	31½	250	9
7	2¾	85	33½	300	10¾
8	3	90	35½	350	12½
9	3½	95	37½	400	14¼
10	4	100	39½	450	16
11	4¼	110	43½	500	17¾
12	4¾	120	47	550	19½
13	5	130	51¼	600	21¼
14	5½	140	55	650	23
15	6	150	59	700	24¾
16	6¼	160	63	750	26½
17	6¾	170	67	800	28¼
18	7	180	70¾	850	30
19	7½	190	74¾	900	31¾
20	8	200	78¾	950	33¾
25	9¾	210	82¾	1000	35½
30	11¾	220	86½	1200	42¼
35	13¾	230	90½	1400	49¼
40	15¾	240	94½	1600	56½
45	17¾	250	98½	1800	63½
50	19¾	300	118	2000	70½

NEEDLE SIZE CONVERSION TABLE

Use the needle size quoted in the patterns as recommended starting points for making a tension sample. The needle size actually used should be that on which you achieve the stated tension.

Metric	US	Old UK
2mm	0	14
2¼mm	1	13
2½mm		
2¾mm	2	12
3mm		
3¼mm	3	10
3½mm	4	
3¾mm	5	9
4mm	6	8
4½mm	7	7
5mm	8	6
5½mm	9	5
6mm	10	4
6½mm	10½	3
7mm		2
7½mm		1
8mm	11	0
9mm	13	00
10mm	15	000

ABBREVIATIONS

alt – alternate
beg – begin(ning)
cm – centimetres
dec – decrease(ing)
foll – follow(ing)
g – grams
in – inch(es)
k – knit
ml – make one stitch by picking up

horizontal loop between stitches and knitting into back of it
mm – millimetres
p – purl
patt – pattern
psso – pass slipped stitch over
rem – remain(ing)
rep – repeat

rnd – round
ssk – slip, slip, knit by slipping 2 stitches separately knitwise, then put left needle 'through front of slipped stitches from left, and knit them together
st(s) – stitch(es)
st.st. – stocking (stockinette) stitch
tog – together

THE ROWAN STORY

We are proud to announce the publication of *The Celtic Collection* by Alice Starmore. A **Rowan Original**, it combines outstanding knitting design with the range and quality of Rowan Yarns.

Rowan is a Yorkshire-based yarn marketing and design company whose name has become synonymous with the revolution that has swept the needlecraft and handkitting industry and changed its image and practice forever. Gone are the limited colours and synthetics offered by most other spinners; we have created a whole new generation of exciting natural-fibre yarns – from kid silk to chenille – in a myriad colours.

Working with the cream of contemporary designers, including Kaffe Fassett, Edina Ronay and Susan Duckworth, Rowan Yarns commissions special handknitting and needlepoint collections, taking what was once a hobby into the realms of high fashion. Rowan's design collections are now in fashion journals worldwide, while every glossy home supplement bears tasteful evidence of Rowan's artistic craftwork.

Home for Rowan is an old stone mill in a narrow green valley in the shadow of the Pennines overlooking Holmfirth. Rowan Yarns was set up just over thirteen years ago by myself and my colleague Simon Cockin. From the beginning our aims were different from our competitors. We took our palette of yarns to top designers; we worked with them to create yarns in colours to match their specific requirements. Some have proved so popular they have become a permanent part of the Rowan range.

Our yarns are now marketed worldwide and the sheer appeal of the variety and subtlety of colours and textures, combined with our willingness to experiment, ensure our continuing success.

The Celtic Collection sets new standards in quality from the very best contemporary designers. The books are produced with the same care and attention that is given to our yarns and the same eye for form and colour that has been our lifelong hallmark. We hope that you will enjoy this new range of original designs using Rowan's yarns.

Stephen Sheard.

YARNS AND SUPPLIERS

The Rowan yarns used for designs throughout this book are named in each pattern and can be obtained from stockists of good quality knitting yarns.

In case of difficulty, write to the addresses below for a list of stockists in your area or consult the yarn list here before substituting a generic equivalent.

4-ply wool	–	Rowan Botany
Heavy 4-ply wool	–	Rowan Lightweight Double Knitting, Rowan Silkstones, Rowan Donegal Lambswool Tweed
Double knitting wool	–	Rowan Designer Double Knitting, Rowan Kid Silk, Rowan Lambswool Tweed
Aran-weight	–	Rowan Chunky Cotton Chenille
4-ply yarn	–	Rowan Wool/Cotton, Rowan Silk/Wool
Double knitting cotton	–	Rowan Fine Cotton Chenille

UNITED KINGDOM
Rowan Yarns Green Lane Mill Holmfirth
West Yorkshire HD7 1RW
Tel 0484 681881
Fax 0484 687920

UNITED STATES OF AMERICA
Westminster Fibers, Inc.
4 Townsend West, Suite 8
Nashua, NH 03063
Tel (603) 886 5041
Fax (603) 886 1056

BELGIUM
Hedera Diestsestraat 172
B – 3000 Leuven
Tel (016) 23 21 89
Fax (016) 23 59 97

CANADA
Estelle Designs and Sales Ltd
Units 65/67 2220 Midland Avenue
Scarborough Ontario M1P 3E6
Tel (416) 298 9922
Fax (416) 298 2429

DENMARK
Designer Garn Vesterbro 33A
DK – 9000 Aalborg
Tel (098) 13 48 24
Fax (098) 13 02 13

FINLAND
Helmi Vuorelma – Oy Vesijarvenkatu 13
SF – 15141 Lahti
Tel (18) 826 831
Fax (18) 517 918

FRANCE
Sidel Mas Tyrex
Route de Beaulieu 13840 Rognes
Tel and Fax 42 50 17 97

GERMANY
Christoph Fritzsch Gmbh
Gewerbepark Dogelmuhle
D – 6367 Karben 1
Tel 06039 2071
Fax 06039 2074

HOLLAND
Henk & Henrietta Beukers
Dorpsstraat 9 NL – 5327 Ar Hurwenen
Tel (04182) 1764
Fax (04182) 2532

ICELAND
Storkurinn Kjorgardi Laugavegi 59
ICE – 101 Reykjavik
Tel (01) 18258
Fax (01) 628252

IRELAND
Needlecraft
27/28 Dawson Street Dublin 2
Tel (01) 772493
Fax (01) 771446

ITALY
La Compagnia Del Cotone
Via Mazzini 44 I – 10123 Torino
Tel (011) 87 83 81
Fax (011) 83 68 68

JAPAN
Diakeito Co Ltd
2-3-11 Senba-Higashi Minoh City
Osaka 562
Tel 0727 27 6604
Fax 0727 27 6654

NEW ZEALAND
John Q Goldingham Ltd
P.O. Box 45083 Epuni Railway Lower Hutt
Tel (04) 5674 085
Fax (04) 5697 444

NORWAY
Eureka
P.O. Box 357 N – 1401 Ski
Tel (09) 871090
Fax (09) 871834

SINGAPORE
The Yarn Garden
126 Joo Seng Road No.07-11
Gold Pine Industrial Building
Singapore 1336
Tel 2883733
Fax 2803449

SWEDEN
Wincent Sveavagen 94
113 50 Stockholm
Tel (08) 673 70 60
Fax (08) 673 31 71

ACKNOWLEDGEMENTS AND SOURCES

ACKNOWLEDGEMENTS

I would like to thank all those involved in the creation of this book, especially Carey Smith of Anaya Publishers and Stephen Sheard of Rowan Yarns for their support and enthusiasm. Thanks also to my editor, Margaret Maino, pattern checker Marilyn Wilson and designer David Fordham. Very special thanks to Karen Harrison, stylist, and Mike Bunn, photographer, for enhancing my designs and producing such beautiful photographs. Finally, but by no means least, I would like to thank my knitters, Jean Downton, Margaret Finlayson, and Peggy Macleod for their many hours of fine work, without which this book would have been a great deal longer in the making.

The picture from the Book of Kells on page 7 is reproduced with the kind permission of The Board of Trinity College, Dublin.

SOURCES

The inspirations for the designs in this book came from the sources listed below.

The Book of Durrow, fifth to sixth century
The Book of Kells, eighth to ninth century
The Book of Lindisfarne, seventh century

For those interested in the study of Celtic Art, I would recommend the following sources:
George Bain, *Celtic Art*, The Methods of Construction, London, Maclellan, 1951
Iain Bain, *Celtic Knotwork*, London, Constable, 1986
Ruth and Vincent Megaw, *Celtic Art* (from the beginnings to The Book of Kells), London, Thames and Hudson, 1989
Frank Delaney, *The Celts*, London, BBC Publications, 1986
Francoise Henry, *The Book of Kells Reproductions from the Manuscript with a Study of the Manuscript*, London, Thames and Hudson, 1974
Michael Ryan, *Treasures of Ireland*, Dublin, Royal Irish Academy, 1983

Butler Area Public Library
218 North McKean Street
Butler, PA 16001